Gaslighting

THE NARCISSIST'S FAVORITE TOOL OF MANIPULATION

How to Avoid the Gaslight Effect and Recover from Emotional and Narcissistic Abuse

Dr. Theresa J. Covert

Table of Contents

Introduction

S arah was a hardworking mother of two boys who decided two months ago that she would quit her day job to start what she cared about; writing her novels.

Recently, her husband, James, has been acting up and complaining that she has not been giving him and their two boys much attention.

She was on her way out to the grocery store earlier today when she noted that her car keys were not on the counter where she always leaves them and decided to ask James about them.

James told Sarah she had put the keys in their bedroom the previous day.

Sarah questioned herself and wondered how on earth she had taken the car keys into the bedroom..."

Has anyone ever told you something that made you doubt your senses?

Well, there are chances that you have been a victim of GASLIGHTING.

Gaslighting, as a term in today's world, isn't what it used

4

to be in the past. Imagine that you were taken back in time to the year 1900, if you picked up a book titled "Gaslighting," you might be doing so to gain knowledge about gas lights which were popular building features powered by gas at that time.

However, "Gaslighting" now refers to a manipulative psychological tactic employed to make someone doubt their sanity. A manipulator tries to get someone to question their reality and perceptions.

Gaslighting occurs in personal relationships, professional relationships, and in some other cases, gaslighting is used by public figures to alter the perceptions of targeted members of the population.

Gaslighting is a form of psychological abuse as it can make you start to doubt your ability to perceive reality correctly. It can make you think you didn't see what you thought you saw or hear what you thought you heard; you start to wonder if you can trust the information you are getting from your five senses. Moreover, this, in turn, will make you begin to think that there must be something wrong with you, and you begin to doubt your sanity.

It doesn't matter whether it is happening in a personal relationship (parent to child, between romantic partners) or a professional relationship at work or even between members of the same community. Gaslighting creates an abusive situation which can cause serious health problems if the victim continues to be in such a position for a long time.

This book does not exclude from its aims the promotion of general awareness of gaslighting as a manipulative tool that can destroy the physical and mental health of individuals. However, it's first aim is that of providing information on how you can understand what gaslighting is precisely and how you can recognize it in your relationships.

No matter whether it occurs in a personal relationship or a working relationship, between a public figure and the members of the public or somewhere else, it's essential to be aware of the signs that you or someone you know might be a victim of gaslighting, as this awareness is the first step to getting out of the negative situation.

The first step to take towards being free from gaslighting is to recognize exactly what gaslighting is as it is often so hard to recognize the signs of gaslighting because the techniques used in gaslighting affect the mind so much that after a long period the victim doesn't even trust their own thoughts.

This book discusses in detail how to distinguish gaslighting behavior from typical behavior by shedding light on the different kinds of gaslighting techniques. And it also aims at providing information about what to do if you find yourself a victim of such a negative situation.

Narcissists are self-centered and arrogant people who lack empathy for others. They live in their own world and believe they are unique and special. Hence, they always seek attention and praise from others.

These groups of people only seek to serve their own needs and won't mind using people as a means for their ends. They don't even think about how their behavior affects others, and this is why they find it so easy to use gaslighting techniques in their relationships.

A narcissist will frequently use gaslighting, as a narcissist's goal is to disorient the victim to gain total control over them. A narcissist achieves this by gradually sowing seeds of doubt in the victim's mind, and in the end, the narcissist controls the victim to do their bidding.

Apart from promoting awareness about gaslighting, this book is written with a more concise aim of exposing the extent to which narcissists as people use gaslighting as a means of manipulation. It is one thing to recognize what gaslighting is, and it is another to know how narcissists operate with it. It is also entirely a different thing to uncover the effects and how to guard yourself against the effects or better still avoid the effects in the first place.

The chapters to come reveal how narcissists seek to control and abuse victims physically and mentally; it exposes the words they say and the actions they take to abuse victims. Also in the chapters to come the harmful effects of gaslighting, empowering strategies for how to disarm narcissists and deal with gaslighting will be discussed to a broader extent.

Chapter 1 - Gaslighting:
The Narcissist's Favorite Tool for Manipulation

What is this thing called gaslighting? How did it come to be the favorite tool of manipulation for a narcissist?

These questions and many more other questions might have come to your mind as you turned to this page, and to understand what gaslighting is, and how it became a favorite tool in a narcissist's tool bag, it is necessary to consider how gaslighting came to be a term.

The term "gaslighting" as a form of emotional abuse came into popular consciousness in a 1938 thriller play written by the British playwright Patrick Hamilton, "Gas Light." The play premiered in London and was adapted later into a movie in 1944. The film was about a husband who tried to convince his wife that she was mentally unstable; his ultimate end was to send her away to a mental asylum so that he could steal her inheritance.

In the movie, the abusive husband, Gregory Anton (depicted by Charles Boyer) manipulates Paula (depicted by Ingrid Bergman) into making her think that she has gone mad. He makes her believe that she is a kleptomaniac without realizing she is, and that she is hearing noises that aren't being heard by any other person.

Paula sees the gas lights around the house dimming at times and brightening at other times for no reason. Unbeknownst to her it was Gregory who was switching the lights on and off to create the impression that she did not see the lights as they were. He was manipulating her belief in her reality.

At a point in the movie, Paula begins to question her reality and thinks she is going crazy through her perception of the gas lights. Gregory's action with the gas lights was one way of how he manipulated her perception of reality.

The movie is a historical reference to the term "Gaslighting" and not all real-life situations are due to a manipulator trying to steal a victim's inheritance.

Real-life gaslighting situations, however, have something in common with what was portrayed in the movie. In "Gaslighting" situations, the goal is to isolate and brainwash the victim to control the victim's version of reality.

Gaslighting happens in several ways in real-life situations; it happens in personal relationships like marriage and friendships; an example is a father always disapproving of his son's decisions to the extent that the son questions decisions he suspects his father would not agree with. The father may want to control every decision made by his son consciously or unconsciously, but he might be gaslighting the son into doubting his own choices.

Another example of gaslighting in personal relationships is that of a spouse who continually humiliates their partner and demands attention from them while putting them down if they refuse to consider them.

Gaslighting also occurs in professional work relationships; a manipulative boss can try to change an employee's perceptions and say things to hurt the employee. A worker can try to bring a subordinate or a coworker down with harmful and destructive words.

Gaslighting happens in television commercial advertisements: a product is advertised, and it leaves you with the feeling that something is wrong with your memory or you are going crazy, and the only way out is for you to buy the product and use it. Public figures, who have a cult-like following, might use their leadership status to mislead the public.

So, what does the term gaslighting mean? "Gaslighting" can be thought of as a verb; we can use it to describe an abusive behavior or action. To be specific, it refers to the behaviors and actions by which a manipulator uses information in such a way as to make a victim question their sanity.

Psychologists define "gaslighting" as a specific type of manipulation where the manipulator tries to get someone else (or a group of people in some cases) to question their reality, memory or perceptions.

Gaslighting is an attempt at convincing a person of something being true by forcefully asserting it or making up flimsy evidence, blatantly denying that one has said something one has said.

It is manipulating another's physical environment to make the person doubt their perceptions or memories about their physical situation. It is intentionally isolating another person from external sources of valid information.

You might come to ask at this point how gaslighting became a favorite tool for narcissists; gaslighting can be intentional sometimes, making someone doubt their memories or perception of reality, to defer to the abuser's account of what reality is. It can be used intentionally to gain authority over a victim's life. Narcissists are known as control freaks, and gaslighting is of no surprise a tool they use in controlling the lives of others.

A narcissist is anyone who suffers from Narcissism Personality Disorder (NPD). The cause of this disorder is not known, but psychologists link NPD to the environment, genetics and neurobiology.

It is essential to understand the behavior of individuals who suffer from NPD because we don't know what a narcissist looks like, the behavior of these individuals is what points them out as narcissists.

A narcissist can be said to be someone who exhibits more than one of the following behavior pattern:

- *Constant Need for Attention and Validation*

Someone who shows a continuous need for attention might be a narcissist, it might be by physically being all over you or constantly saying words to demand your attention. Narcissists can't self-validate, and so they continuously look for other people to approve of them and no matter what others say to validate them, they never feel it is enough, and will always want more. No matter how much you say "I love you" or "I admire you" to a narcissist, they never feel it is enough. They continually attempt to evoke recognition and endorsement from others to support their delicate self-image, but regardless of the amount they are given, they always need more.

- *Demand for Control all the Time*

Narcissists will demand that you say and do precisely what they have in mind so that they can achieve their ideal goals. A narcissist sees you internally as a character in their own script, not a genuine individual with your own thoughts and sentiments.

When you don't behave as a narcissist expects you to behave, they become very disturbed because they don't know what to expect from you next as you are now operating outside of their scripts.

The need for control stems out of the narcissist's ideals. Narcissists don't want to believe life is imperfect and they want to control and mold life into what they envision, so they always want to be in control of everything.

- *Entitlement*

The narcissist sees themselves at the top of the world with everyone beneath their feet. In their heads, they are entitled to the best, and they have to be the best, the richest, the greatest and so on.

By being entitled, they don't see the world for what it is; they see the world in binary, either good or bad, and they are either superior or inferior beings. They feel everything

14

must be done their way and they must own and control everyone.

- *Perfectionism*

Is there anyone in your life who believes everything should be perfect and is dissatisfied continuously when life doesn't play out the way they envisioned it?

The narcissist has an extremely high need for everything to be perfect. They believe they should be perfect, you should be perfect, events should happen exactly as they expected. This is an excruciatingly impossible demand, which results in the narcissist feeling dissatisfied and miserable much of the time.

- *Refusing Responsibility*

At the point when things don't go as planned, the narcissist blames all faults on others. It must always be another person's deficiency and not theirs. To keep up the façade of flawlessness, narcissists consistently need to accuse some other person or a thing.

- *Absence of empathy*

Narcissists have next to no capacity of empathizing with others. They are too self-absorbed to comprehend what other individuals are feeling. They are also rarely apologetic, remorseful, or guilty.

Narcissists likewise come up short on a comprehension about the idea of emotions. They don't see how their feelings happen. They think their emotions are brought about by a person or thing outside of themselves. They don't understand that their emotions are brought about by their very own natural chemistry and thought patterns. This absence of sympathy makes genuine relationships with narcissists very difficult. They simply don't see what any other individuals are feeling.

- *Invulnerability*

Narcissists are quick to jump from one relationship to the next because they desperately want someone to identify with them and feel their pains but are not willing to respond to the feelings of the other person.

The reason for this is that it takes a little vulnerability to keep relationships. Relationships are all about caring and sharing, because of the narcissist's inability to understand feelings, their lack of empathy, and constant need for self-security, narcissists can't genuinely love or connect on an emotional level with other people. They cannot see the world from anyone else's perspective.

- *Inability to work as part of a team.*

Being insightful and cooperating with other people requires a genuine comprehension of other's feelings. A narcissist can't genuinely understand other peoples' feelings and won't give anything up for the benefit of others.

Narcissists are also compulsive liars who will go to great lengths to gain power and control over others. The willingness to do anything just to control the actions of others makes gaslighting easy for them to use, and since gaslighting is lying with a goal, the goal of the narcissist is to gain control over the action of another.

Narcissists will use shame and confusion to isolate victims. The narcissist's goal is often to make the target entirely dependent on them alone, and in a bid to control the victim they will incite fear with words and actions that will make the victim withdraw from loved ones. This withdrawal from loved ones makes it easy for narcissists to abuse victims even more as there is no third-party present to rescue the victims.

Narcissists have a compulsive need to be perfect people at all times, so gaslighting comes in handy in making other peoples' perception of an event a wrong one and to show and convince others that they are right at all time.

In going to great lengths and doing anything to get their object of desire, narcissists often step on others. Moreover, when they are confronted for their misdoings, they resolve to tactics to minimize or erase what they have done and won't hesitate to abuse people to get to this end, making people think that how they feel about having their toes stepped on is totally unimportant.

This is another form of abuse in itself as narcissists may use gaslighting to fabricate conversations and events that never happened.

Healthy people display noble acts of selflessness from time to time, but since the world revolves around narcissists, they are always about their feelings and needs, so they employ tactics to dismiss the feelings and needs of others.

Narcissists also love to evade responsibility, and they renege on agreements or promises they have previously made.

Master manipulators like narcissists can play on people's emotions; they play the victim to evoke sympathy, love, and support for themselves from others. They won't hesitate to use gaslighting to present themselves as persons in pain to sap the feelings of others.

Gaslighting over time effectively disconnects the victim

from themselves, their feelings, and their ability to decide and know what they want for themselves.

As gaslighting progress, the victim of abuse will often second-guess their thoughts. Doubting their thoughts may put them on the defensive and prevent them from criticizing the narcissist's behavior. This self-doubt can give the narcissist more opportunity to manipulate the victim.

Eventually, gaslighting strips the victim of self-identity, the very core of the victim and leaves them feeling dependent on the narcissist, so the narcissist takes control of their lives and provides approval for them about what reality is.

It doesn't matter whether it's happening in a marriage, or at work or somewhere else, it is vital to be aware of the signs that you (or someone you know) might be a victim. This awareness is the first step to getting out of this abusive situation.

Gaslighting can cause long-term negative effects on the victim's psychological health, and it takes specialized help to restore the victim's balanced sense of self. Gaslighting only works when the victims are not aware of what is happening, but once they catch what is happening, they can take proactive steps to produce lasting changes.

To effect long-lasting changes, however, doesn't come easy. In a childhood memoir titled *An Abbreviated Life,* Ariel Leve tells of how she grew up on the Upper West Side of New York City with a narcissistic mother who lived a very privileged life. Ariel tells of how her mother partied with Andy Warhol and some other prominent personalities of that era, picked physical fights with her boyfriends and yelled at her and always called her "an ungrateful child." She wrote of the horrible abuses she went through as a child and how her childhood was filled with loneliness, chaos, and fear. In interviews about her childhood memoir, Ariel always comments about how hard it was for her to get over memories of the abuse and how her mother consistently denied that it took place, a fact she would always talk about in interviews about her memoirs as "an erasure of the abuse which was even worse than the abuse itself".

It is essential to realize that anyone and any relationship can be a victim of gaslighting, though it is easier to notice gaslighting in romantic relationships because the end goal is often to gain control.

In the end, narcissists often get what they want, and in relating with people at work or in the community, it might be hard to detect gaslighting because for the most part in these situations the goal might not only be to control, it might be other things, money as an example.

The adverse effects of gaslighting can linger on in the victim's mind for a long time, but it is possible to recognize gaslighting at an early stage and avoid the consequences of this form of abuse, which is the subject of the next chapter.

Chapter 2 – What Is Gaslighting? | How to Avoid Mental Manipulation

The preceding chapter presented gaslighting as a form of manipulation that seeks to sow the seeds of doubt into a targeted individual's mind, and as a form of manipulation that makes the victim question their memory, perception, and sanity.

By misdirecting victims, saying contradictory words and lying, gaslighting is done in subtle ways so that the victims don't realize what is being done to them, as they are persistently denied of what is real.

Gaslighting is an attempt to destabilize a victim to gain total control over them, and we have already established it as a favorite tool for manipulators like narcissists who are control freaks.

Narcissists use gaslighting as a psychological manipulation technique for their benefit, by deliberately trying to alter other people's perception of reality, creating an imbalance of power and exploiting victims to serve their purposes.

Some signs and symptoms reveal that you (or someone you know) are manipulated with gaslighting. I would like you to take a minute to ask yourself if any of these scenarios are right for you or someone you know.

- *You find yourself withholding valuable information from your friends, and family, so they don't have a clue of what's going on with you or you make excuses for what's going on with you.*

- *You feel something is not right with you as you are always being criticized by your partner/boss/friend/co-worker or parent.*

- *You have been wondering of late if you are good enough as a girlfriend/wife/employee /son/daughter/parent/because your boyfriend/girlfriend/boss/father/mother/husband/co-worker continually puts you down.*

- *You feel like someone is sucking the joy out of your life.*

- *You are constantly second-guessing yourself.*

- *You feel crazy and confused.*

- *You are always told by a*

spouse/boss/parent/co-worker that you are too
sensitive, and something is wrong with you.
- *You are misremembering things of late.*

- *You are continually saying sorry for things as*
  you don't trust what you think again.

There might be a chance you (or someone you know) are caught in a gaslighting situation if any of these things seem to be happening to you. If you find more than three of these scenarios valid for you, then it is time for you to take a step back and assess your situation. It is time to evaluate all your relationships, both personal and professional.

Mental manipulation can have damaging effects on victims. You must have noticed a particular person you relate with seemed to get whatever they want, whenever they want it. Have you looked at this person with admiration, and yet, with a bit of disgust because you feel they didn't get the things they got in the right way?

All things considered, if you felt like they were exploiting you or other people, you are most likely right because narcissists are master manipulators who seek to control people at work, life, and relationships.

It is hard to spot the ways that someone might be using others for their own advantage, but there are ways to recognize it and even stop it before it happens. Mental manipulation allows abusers to take from others for their own benefit as it works in a way to make victims lose control of their minds and become vulnerable to the will of the abuser.

If you recognize a pattern of certain kinds of anomaly in your relationships, and you are starting to see ways in which you are being manipulated into doubting what your reality is, then it's about time you take proactive steps to avoid further mental manipulation and emotional abuse because ultimately you might step down into a state of utter depression if you decide not to do anything about your situation.

So how do you avoid the mental manipulation and emotional abuse caused by gaslighting?

1.   *You have to develop an unwavering belief in your intuition.*

It can be really challenging for someone who has been under the control of a narcissist to start listening to their intuition; this is because the narcissist has been telling them not to believe their intuition for some time.

Sitting in silence for a set portion of time in a day practicing meditation can help to silence the mind and still the body so that the truth of the situation can be sought out. By taking deep breaths, you'd come to see how a narcissist has been gaslighting you and as time passes your intuition will come alive much more, and you will start trusting it.

When you listen to yourself and your feelings, and you feel self-doubt or confusion lurking around inside you, question why exactly you feel that way. Pay attention to the actions and words of the people you relate with daily. Then you will be able to notice the inconsistencies in their words and actions. It is necessary to develop an unwavering belief in your intuition as trusting your gut will help you to understand and be aware of what is going on around you.

2.   *You have to know your fundamental human rights*

As long as you are not causing harm to others, you have the right to stand up for yourself. Some of our fundamental human rights as humans are the rights to:

Express our feelings and opinions;

Be treated with respect;

Set our goals and determine our priorities; and

Create our own healthy and happy lives, among others.

Of course, society is full of people who do not respect these fundamental human rights. Psychological manipulators such as narcissists, in particular, want to deprive people of their rights so they can control and take advantage of them but when you know your rights, you will have every right to declare that it is you, who's in charge of your life and not anyone else.

Be assertive for yourself. Start by choosing to stop responding to words and actions the way you did before, speak up, and don't be afraid to say no to things or people that seek to manipulate you.

3.   *You have to let go of self-blame*

The narcissist's agenda is to look for ways to make you think you are crazy so that they can have their way and when you realize that you are caught up in a gaslighting situation, it is understandable that you may feel non-worthy, or even blame yourself for not satisfying the narcissist.

Understand that you are not a problem. If you have realized you are being manipulated, that is no fault of yours in any way. Be aware that you did nothing wrong to cause it and that it is the other person that has their problems. However, don't let this lead to self-pity and self-blame.

In situations like these, it's important to remember that you are not the problem; you're being manipulated to feel that you are insane so that you surrender your power and rights. Self-blame can lead to more problems and give the narcissist an edge in the situation to abuse you more.

4.   *You can keep your distance*

You have to understand that when you're in a situation with someone who is gaslighting you, you're never going to be able to convince them of your view of things. It is best that you escape with your brain intact and be willing to move on with your own life. Allow yourself to escape this situation with your sanity intact. A narcissistic person won't change, so it is best to keep your distance if you can.

Emotional abuse that occurs in personal relationships can be much harder to avoid. Think about your relationship with the other person. Maybe you want to speak with friends about how you feel, or perhaps you want to confront the person. Consider all the options and do what is okay for you.

You can take back the control of your senses by confronting them if you do not believe you are in harm's way. You should know that explaining how you feel and what is bothering you is not doing anything wrong. Request that the other person changes their behavior and how they talk to you. Don't let them continue with the same actions. Take your power back and do what you need to do.

Also, know that people who manipulate others don't change easily. So, in doing what is okay for you do not try to change anyone who you suspect might be a narcissist or anyone you know to be a manipulator. Know that their behavior is hard-wired to their brains and trying to change them on your own might well be a waste of your time and efforts. Leave such relationships if you can.

Chapter 3 – Cognitive Dissonance | How Manipulation Affects You

B efore we take a more in-depth look into how narcissists operate to make you think you are crazy, it is essential to introduce the concept of cognitive dissonance as this will further shed light on how narcissists work to make their victims feel mad. A brief digression into this concept will aid our understanding of how manipulation works.

Cognitive dissonance is a term used to describe the feelings of discomfort. This discomfort occurs when a person holds contradictory ideas or beliefs in their minds at the same time.

In psychology, cognitive dissonance is a theory centered on how people try to reach a state of inner consistency; cognitive dissonance is the psychological stress experienced by a person who holds two contradictory beliefs or ideas in mind. A psychologist named Leon Festinger first proposed the theory.

He proposed that people have an inner need to ensure that what their beliefs are and what their behaviors are, are consistent. When there an inconsistency, state of internal disharmony arises, and this state is something people strive to avoid.

In relationships, cognitive dissonance is one of the results of emotional abuse used by narcissists; they cause cognitive dissonance to create in the victim a sense of confusion. Mental manipulation by narcissists comes subtly, and cognitive dissonance is one of the side effects of being emotionally abused in a relationship with a narcissist.

Let's take a little time here to continue with the story of Sarah, the hardworking mother of two boys who was accused by her husband that she is giving too much attention to what she is passionate about – writing her novels.

The story continues with James telling Sarah when she came back from the grocery store that he couldn't believe she was wasting her time writing novels and that she was selfish and only cares about herself. Sarah's feelings were hurt, and she begins to think for a while that maybe she is too insensitive and shouldn't be pursuing her passion after all.

Unbeknownst to her, her husband, a narcissist, has been gaslighting her. She begins to doubt her guts, and she starts growing confused; at this point she had begun to hold the belief that she was insensitive.

When the time came for dinner, Sarah raised the fact that she loved writing her novels, and she has in no way stopped giving attention to James and the boys. James said no one has ever said she was not giving them attention and that she is "crazy" for thinking that.

So, like Sarah, have you been struggling inside your mind and dealing with conflicting thoughts? You wanted to take a course of action, but someone said something that pulled you towards a new direction? That is the essence of cognitive dissonance.

Cognitive dissonance is not what a narcissist does, it is the result of the narcissist's emotional abuse, and it all happens in the victim's mind. Cognitive dissonance is one of the side effects of being in a relationship with a narcissist. It comes in forms of brain fogs, and it feels like a carousel is spinning around inside your head. It is a state of emotional dizziness, as your thoughts and actions are not in harmony. The narcissist uses gaslighting to drive a victim into a state of cognitive dissonance.

It is essential to note at this point that cognitive dissonances do not only occur in abusive relationships, but also happens in real-life situations as we make decisions in day-to-day life.

In typical real-life situations, people reduce the magnitude of their cognitive dissonance by changing their behavior or their mental perception of a thing; people also reduce the extent of their cognitive dissonance by justifying their actions and adding more viewpoints, or they deny any information that contrasts with information they already hold.

However, in personal and work relationships, it can often be challenging to reduce the magnitude of cognitive dissonance or overcome it. This is because it's hard to believe that your boss/husband/co-worker/spouse or parent might be trying to abuse you, or you have invested so much in a relationship that it becomes so hard for you to accept the fact that gaslighting is happening.

In manipulative situations, the victim might not realize that the cognitive dissonance they feel is as a result of gaslighting by the narcissist, because they are too emotionally or financially invested in the abusive relationship.

By now we know a narcissist will use all sorts of gaslighting tactics to put the victim into a state of dependency, and to survive the ordeal, the victim will unconsciously employ different mechanisms. One of these coping mechanisms is cognitive dissonance.

Perhaps you have identified with some things discussed in this chapter, and you have remembered times when you have experienced cognitive dissonance. The good thing is that cognitive dissonance that results from narcissistic gaslighting can be erased. However, it is pertinent to note at this junction that there are both healthy and unhealthy ways to deal with cognitive dissonance.

The unhealthy ways to remove cognitive dissonance will make the victim fall into further abuse by the narcissist, and the cycle of mental manipulation will continue. These unhealthy ways are:

Evasion: which is where the victim is fully aware of what is happening but doesn't want to acknowledge it and creates a sense of denial about what is happening by evading what is right and refusing to change thoughts and beliefs which will eventually remove the dissonance.

Refusing change: is when you refuse to let go of your current thoughts and beliefs. Cognitive dissonance will disappear after a while of adhering to your current thinking patterns.

Seeking the validation of negative influences: trying to remove cognitive dissonance by seeking validation from toxic people will only reinforce the cognitive dissonance in the long run.

The healthy ways to deal with cognitive dissonance are:

Writing in a Journal Frequently:

Cognitive dissonance often is a symptom of an underlying issue. When you experience the symptoms, it is time to analyze your thoughts and question them.

Writing down the thoughts in your head on paper can make you more self-aware, and you can see the conflicts in your thoughts as you go back to your entries.

Writing in a diary or some other type of private, contemplative writing can be a valuable tool for investigating and settling those conflicting thoughts and delivering a feeling of mental clarity and ease.

Speaking to trusted people:

Let people who care about you know of your troubles if you realize a narcissist is psychologically manipulating you. Trusted friends and family are good people who have your best interests at heart, and you can count on them for positive support.

You might also consult your spiritual adviser when you think someone is manipulating you. Positive support counts and when you speak to the people you trust, you get a lot off your mind and gain new perspectives on your issues of concern.

Talking to a therapist:

If you can't find someone close to confide in it is best you speak to a licensed therapist.

Therapy is well known as a tool for overcoming addictions, anxiety, and depression. It helps you manage your emotions and see things from a different perspective.

Talking to a therapist will help you get a feeling of how you appear to other individuals, and you get feedback on your emotions along with understanding how your feelings affect you from day to day.

Eliminating cognitive dissonance is not always an easy undertaking, but it's worth it. It takes consistent attention to working on yourself and creating more self-awareness.

Using healthy ways to deal with cognitive dissonance will make you be at peace with yourself, and you will rediscover your power to act according to the beliefs you hold.

It takes a lot of work to deal with the cognitive dissonance that results from emotional abuse, but it goes a long way to help you overcome mental manipulation and live a peaceful and healthy life.

Chapter 4 – How Gaslighting Narcissists Operate to Make their Victim Think that they are Crazy

We have already established that gaslighting does not only occur in personal relationships but also in professional-work relationships and relationships with members of the community. Also, we have seen how gaslighting is a favorite tool for a narcissist and how to avoid mental manipulation by a narcissist.

It cannot be stressed enough that gaslighting can damage a victim's mental and emotional health, and it works well for the narcissist because they can manipulate in the subtlest ways. When narcissists are confronted for their acts of manipulation, they can prove that it is the victim who is the crazy one. This might be believable because most times, victims will not even have the proof that they are being manipulated.

Narcissists use gaslighting to gain control over their victims, and when the victims cannot prove that the narcissist said or acted in a way, they often go back to the narcissist for what reality is, or they hold the narcissist's version of events as real.

So, what are the cues narcissists pick up to drive their victims crazy? How does a narcissist operate to make their victims crazy? To understand how narcissists use gaslighting to make victims think they are crazy, it is necessary to look into a few things narcissists do and say before we paint a bigger picture of how they operate.

The narcissist will twist words to create images in the mind of the victim. In a bid to make the victim question what their reality is all about, the narcissist will say things about the victim's life, friends, family, possessions, among other topics.

Saying things about a victim's primary relationships is one of the ways a narcissist will seek to manipulate the victim. This is the very first maneuver a narcissist will use to make victims think that they are crazy.

Not only will narcissists say words that will make their victims doubt their mother, father, siblings, or best friends, narcissists will go further to make victims question the intentions of the people that care so much about them. This happens because the narcissist wants to isolate their victims so that they can gain total control over their lives. They also perceive people who love the victims as obstacles to their plans.

Why would a narcissist seek to do this evil thing? Well, narcissists are aware that the victim's loved ones will always support them and will bring them back to a state of sanity so not only will narcissists question the intentions of the victim's loved ones, narcissists will drop subtle accusations about a victim's loved ones so as to create a breach of trust.

Another way a narcissist will make the victim think they are crazy is by projecting their negative actions at the victim. A narcissist is never at fault with anything, and hence they will project their actions onto their victims when they are confronted for any wrongdoing. Even when a narcissist makes a mistake, instead of admitting it was their mistake, they will turn it over on the victim. The victim is always responsible.

Many times, when narcissists are caught doing exactly what they said they would not do by the victims, they magically turn the tables and all of a sudden, the victims are held responsible for their wrongdoing.

Narcissists do not only project their wrong actions on others, but they project lies too, and when they are confronted for lying, they can turn it around to make it seem that it was the victim who was lying or it was the victim who made them lie.

Let's take a break here to consider an example portrayed

by the story of a well-raised child who left home for college and made all the wrong choices in college, dropped out and then returns home to put all the blame on his parents. This is an example of a narcissistic child who is refusing to take responsibility for his actions. Instead, he is blaming the parents who have done their all to raise a good child.

Apart from saying the wrong words about their victim's relationships and putting the blame of their misdeeds on the victims, another way through which narcissists seek to make their victim think they are crazy is through mismatching words and deeds. They say a thing and go on to do another thing.

It is easy for a gaslighting narcissist to say one thing and do another. This is because a narcissist is a great salesperson who can get a victim to invest in them emotionally. A narcissist is the kind of person who will tell a victim continually "I love you" but will never go out of their way to be there or show that they genuinely love the victim.

Narcissists will make promises and never back them up, and when the victims are too emotionally invested in them, they will think that maybe one day the narcissist will follow through on their promise. This waiting on their commitment can put the victim into a psychological mess as their sense of identity and self-esteem are attached to a lie.

However, it is essential to note that there are times when narcissists intentionally show acts of kindness, and this is another way in which they seek to manipulate the victim to think they are crazy. They keep victims confused when they in the midst of all their gaslighting acts by doing something that seems to be selfless to the victim.

These random acts of kindness are just hooks to draw the victim deeper and deeper into confusion, and they do this when they realize the victim is about to pull away from the deception. After they have used gaslighting on their victims for a while, they do something outstanding and declare that they are well-meaning.

At this point, it is worthy to note that there are times when victims present cues that make it easy for the narcissist to continue to manipulate and control their reality. So, what are the signals narcissists pick up on to manipulate their victims to think they are crazy?

1. *The victim displays an emotional or relational vulnerability*

Psychological vulnerabilities like past hurts, needs, or emotions can expose a victim to gaslighting from a narcissist. As a result of talking to the narcissists on a personal level, they might give out too much information that can make the narcissist step over them. While trying to make the victim sound crazy, a narcissist might say something like "How did you come to a conclusion like that?" The narcissist will do this intentionally so that the victim starts to second-guess themselves.

2. *The victim reveals a personal issue of concern*

Similar to displaying an emotional vulnerability, revealing wishes, desires and a bit of the inner person by a victim can predispose them to a gaslighting narcissist who could see this information as an opportunity to give wrong advice or interpretations to confuse the victim.

3. *The victim makes an error or a miscalculation*

This happens in professional relationships in most cases, making mistakes is a normal part of life, but narcissists can exploit the fact that others make a mistake to manipulate them.

It comes as no surprise when you learn that narcissists are hyper-vigilant and too often, they possess good memories to keep track of another person's life. So, when a narcissist knows you made a little mistake, they can come around to say words that will bring you down.

4. The victim tries to create harmony

This is when a victim approaches a narcissist with the mind of creating a win-win situation for both the narcissist and the victim. Unknown to most victims, narcissists will only seek to win for themselves and might use such cases to an unfair advantage. It can also happen in a situation where the victim realizes their mistake and tries to seek the forgiveness of a narcissist.

5. The victim is trying to be helpful

The gaslighting narcissists will still find faults with a kind person. They do not have empathy and will always look for an angle to pounce on their victim.

Narcissists will look for any of these cues to disorientate their victim and make them think they are crazy. To put all these together, we can bring the ways narcissists operate together in an umbrella of terms:

- **Baiting**

Baiting means luring the victim with a false sense of security. By pretending to be good listeners which they never are, narcissist learns about the victim's flaws and insecurities and will use this knowledge later on to provoke the victim.

Provoking the victim is just a bait, and if the victim truly gets angry, the narcissist will talk about how they did not mean to make the victim angry. In this way, they will manipulate the victim to think they did not intend to hurt them.

- **Love Bombing**

Love bombing often occurs in the early phases of a relationship.

Gaslighting narcissists will often operate in this way. Love bombing implies that the narcissists overwhelm the victim with attention, flattery, compliments, or romance.

It looks good to be showered with attention on the surface, but what the victim does not know is that the gestures are made to manipulate them further.

Love bombs are the activities aimed at gaining your affection and trust. When a narcissist knows they have your faith, they are in charge and will start to control you to get what they need.

Narcissists as mentioned earlier in this book, will struggle to maintain mutually beneficial relationships, because at the end of the day, they only want the relationship to benefit themselves, and after some time, you will be left in obscurity to recuperate your enthusiastic injuries.

So here lies another problem. It tends to be extremely hard to see love bombing when it is happening; but here are signs that indicate love bombing.

1. *Everything is happening way too fast*

A narcissist will fall in love with you or display signs of affection to you more quickly than you have ever experienced before. They will make you have a feeling that you're flawless. They may even reveal to you that you're the love of their lives they have been waiting for. Not too long after they meet you, they are showering you with gifts.

That doesn't mean you can't trust a new relationship, but that you ought to be careful of any relationship that seems to appear unexpectedly out of nowhere. When it comes to falling in love with someone, the narcissist makes the magic seem real, but the reality is much different.

Know for a fact that true love grows slowly and recognize when things are moving too fast.

2. You are always being asked about the things that don't seem to be working in your life.

When you notice someone who just entered your life is always curious to know the things you have difficulties with or the things that don't seem to be working in your life, then be careful of such a person. A narcissist will continuously ask you such questions because they want to provide solutions for you so that you think they are the savior that has finally come to rescue you.

What you might not observe is that they are curious so that you think of how awesome they are, and also, they are storing more information about you to be used against you later on in the relationship.

3. They disrespect other people.

This is a great way to know a person is a narcissist. Narcissists will treat other people like crap, especially people they perceive are of lower status than themselves. When you are with a narcissist, and someone else comes

If you observe this in a relationship and you notice it is a pattern that repeats itself, then you need to get away as quickly as possible.

4. Nothing feels steady in the relationship

Later on, in your new relationship, you might start to experience a never-ending cycle of emotions. One moment you feel great, then the next moment you start feeling like a terrible human being. Healthy relationships don't go this way, most parts of healthy relationships are stable.

That's what a narcissist does, and they are quite skilled at it: when they compliment you, you feel like the best person in the world and then later they will put you down, abuse you and make you feel like the worst person in the world.

- **Covert threats**

"Do this or I will do that."

Covert threats happen when a victim challenges a notion or demand of a narcissist, the narcissist has a false sense of superiority and will see themselves as superiors who should not be challenged, so when the victim does not live up to their expectation or challenges them in any way, they feel threatened and attempt to instill fear.

In the event that somebody's response to you having a contrasting opinion from their own is to threaten you into submission, regardless of whether it is a subtle threat or an unmistakable confirmation of what they intend to do, this is a warning sign that the person has a false sense of superiority.

Rather than solve disagreements maturely, narcissists will redirect to an attempt to instill fear in you about what will happen if you do not choose to comply with them.

When someone threatens you in any way, pay attention and let them know you mean business by standing up for yourself, record their threats, and report them when possible.

- **Name-calling**

Name-calling is another resort for gaslighting narcissists. It is an easy way with which they put victims down, so a gaslighting narcissist won't hesitate to call the behavior of the victim "stupid" or "dumb" just to insult the victim's intelligence and degrade them.

Name-calling is one of the last techniques gaslighting narcissists resort to when they can't think of a better way to invalidate your opinion. It is the easiest way to put you down as a victim. Name-calling is also used to degrade your intelligence and appearance.

Rather than addressing a current issue, a narcissist will

target you as a person because they feel threatened as only they are right. When a narcissist calls you all sorts of negative things, it is best for you not to internalize them and realize that they are seeking to undermine you because of their grandiose sense of self-importance.

- **Shaming**

"You should be ashamed of yourself..."

This is one of the favorite sayings of a gaslighting narcissist. When a narcissist feels challenged in any way, they use shaming to hit at their victim's self-esteem. They can do this because they know about abuse or an injustice a victim has suffered in the past. They enjoy opening past wounds to retraumatize victims to make them feel unworthy.

Shaming is essentially an attempt at making you feel lesser than yourself by the narcissist.

In the event that you suspect you are relating with a narcissist, abstain from revealing any of your vulnerabilities or past injuries. Don't show anything from your past to people who have not convinced you of their good characters.

- **Condescending Jokes**

Gaslighting narcissists enjoy making malicious jokes at the expense of the victim, so they get away with saying abusive things in the form of jokes and will often accuse the victim of having no sense of humor when they are confronted.

Narcissists will use these kinds of jokes in gaslighting the victim, and in the end, the victim knows they have been abused by the narcissists but will still think it was just a joke after all.

Narcissists will also use sarcasm to tear the victim down, and if the victim reacts, they will label them as "sensitive." This will drive the victim into always double-checking their thoughts before they express them in words and they will begin to silence themselves.

- **Control**

Gaslighting narcissists are control freaks who want to control anything they can in the victim's life. They want to manage every facet of the victim's life; their finances, their friends, their time, their hobbies, and so on.

They want control because the more power they have over the victim, the more the victim will rely on them.

- **Triangulation**

"Even (name) thinks you are crazy."

Triangulation is bringing in the opinion or perspective of a third party into a relationship. In romantic relationships, triangulation can also stand for bringing in another person to form a love triangle so that the victim can feel insecure. Narcissists use other people's opinion to approve of their own perspectives.

Narcissists often triangulate their partners in romantic relationships with strangers, colleagues, friends, and relatives to evoke jealousy. This is a diversionary strategy intended to pull the victim away from the abusive situation and paint a false image of themselves as a desirable person.

Also to create a confusing effect in the mind of the victim, narcissists make up other people's false opinions and project it onto their victims, so if a narcissist has been telling a victim "you are crazy" for a while, the narcissist might come at a later date say "Even your co-worker, (name) says you are crazy."

- **Nitpicking**

Nitpicking means continually finding faults in others and criticizing little things others do.

Narcissists are often perfectionists who want everything in life to turn out perfectly and so they are quick to find fault in people and things.

Are you a millionaire? The narcissist will then start to pick on you and ask you why you aren't a multi-millionaire yet.

A narcissist will always raise the bar higher and higher; a narcissist seeks to instill in you a sense of never being good enough, even when they don't raise their expectations for you, they might shift their expectations for you completely. They do all these to create a feeling of unworthiness in you.

At work, a narcissist will criticize you and say their motive is to help you improve and be the best, but they just w

ant to nitpick and make you the scapegoat when things don't turn out well. Even in the case of meeting their set targets, the narcissist will still find reasons to be dissatisfied with you.

When you argue with a narcissist, and you have presented all the evidence that could validate you, a narcissist will still demand more proof and bring in matters not relevant to the matter of contention. They do this by pointing out one irrelevant fact or one thing you did wrong and then change the whole context of the argument.

Gaslighting narcissists will use these techniques to make their victims think that they are crazy. They do this in subtle ways you can't easily recognize, so it is hard to see what they are really up to.

Gradually, the effects of gaslighting starts to set in in the victim, and the victim experiences cognitive dissonance, and after continuous gaslighting, the victim starts to question their sanity and think they are actually going crazy.

Let's look at the effects of gaslighting.

Chapter 5 – The Effects
of Gaslighting

Gaslighting is a crazy-making effect that can lead to exploitation, which is sometimes hard to see. The intention of the person using gaslighting is to, in a subtle and organized way, crumble the self-confidence of the victim so that they are not able to act independently. In the end, the victim becomes a robot who only obeys the order of the manipulator.

The emotional damage caused by gaslighting can be enormous on the victim. When a person is exposed to gaslighting for too long, they lose their sense of self-identity, and they start to distrust their judgment and second-guess themselves.

Gaslighting may lead a victim to develop emotional and mental concerns. The self-doubting and confusion can add to anxiety, and this anxiety can lead to depression, post-traumatic stress, and codependency.

The effects of gaslighting can be detrimental on the victim; these effects don't come all at once; they come in three stages: disbelief, defense, and depression. Before we go into these stages, let's take a look at the harmful effects gaslighting has on victims;

1. Confusion

Gaslighting works when the victim is unaware of it, and the constant use of gaslighting tactics by the narcissist makes the victim gradually bend to their will. Over time, doubts creep into the mind of the victims, and with more gaslighting going on, the victim is confused by what is going on. Though they know something is going wrong, they can't pinpoint exactly what it is.

It is a never-ending cycle for the victims as long as they are in close relation with the narcissist. Confusion results from the narcissist's exploitation of the victim's vulnerabilities. Narcissists keep their victims always second-guessing what they throw at them as they are always alternating between acts of cruelty and acts of kindness.

The narcissists break down victims piece by piece so that they become more and more unstable, and eventually, victims come to rely on them for comfort and guidance as confusion takes its toll on victims mentally and physically.

Confusion in the victims eventually leads to isolation, as the victims are too confused as to how the whole situation came to be in the first place.

2. Loss of confidence.

When a person falls victim of a gaslighting narcissist, their confidence starts to erode, and as they may find themselves second-guessing things, the victim develops a heightened sense of self-doubt. Every decision will now be backed with an internal question, *"What if I...?"*

The victims start to live in fear of doing the wrong things as they are now sensitive to the constant projection, blame, lies, and humiliation of the narcissist. As a result of looking up to the narcissist for approval before taking actions, they ask themselves *"Am I too sensitive....?"* And because they act with fear, they often end up making mistakes in their activities.

As time progresses, the victim will start showing the signs of low confidence; they would find it hard to offer a simple thank you when they are complimented. This happens because of the unconscious emotional damage caused by gaslighting: a victim will reject a positive view of themselves because they have unconsciously accepted the fact that they are unworthy from the narcissist.

A victim will find it hard to hold eye contact with others because they are afraid others will see right through them and notice their flaws. The narcissists have successfully projected a part of themselves onto the victim.

Loss of confidence also makes victims always apologize as they are never doing anything right in the eyes of the narcissist and to prevent further name-calling and humiliation, they apologize even for the words they say.

3. Indecision

A typical result of gaslighting is questioning *everything,* as the victim doesn't know what's real and what's imagined. This, in turn, means the victim finds it challenging to make the most straightforward choices because they now find it impossible to know what is "right" from what is "wrong".

Victims of gaslighting not only have trouble making big decisions, but simple choices such as brushing their teeth are now also hard to make, as they have been caught up in the narcissist's web of illusion, and they are bonded to the narcissist.

This kind of bond to the narcissist is formed out of the fear that the victim will lose their sense of self. One part of the victim will try to align itself to the needs and choices of the narcissist, while another will try to align itself with the victim's preferences.

Moreover, the narcissist projects their fear of taking responsibility, and the need for perfection onto the victim, so the fear of taking responsibility makes it hard to make decisions.

Gradually, victims begin to lose their power to make decisions until they are unable to decide anything for themselves. Now they have to rely on the narcissist for guidance and ask the narcissist for permission to do things.

4. Distrust

As a result of the shame victims of gaslighting feel, they try to cover up the fact that mental manipulation is going on in their lives and when their family and best friends start to notice the changes in them, they deny the subject and cover-up, or they may avoid the issue.

Gaslighting victims start to withhold information from people who mean well because they live in fear of what will happen if they were ever found out by the narcissist. They begin to withdraw from society, and they start to distrust other people.

The victims of gaslighting not only have trouble trusting family and friends but they also increasingly feel they can't trust themselves either.

Distrust causes victims not only an inability to form new friendships and relationships but also to withdraw themselves into isolation from friends and family.

This particular effect of gaslighting continues to take place even after the victim has successfully eliminated the narcissist from their lives as when they make new friends, they find it difficult to trust and will always be hypervigilant about relationships.

5. Melancholy

Gaslighting practiced on the victim over time will take away the happiness and joy of the victims. Narcissists leave their victims afraid, confused, lonely, and unhappy through mental manipulation and emotional abuse.

The victims have the feeling that they used to be a different person; one who was confident and carefree. What the victims don't realize is that anyone who lives under the constant oppression of the gaslighting narcissist can have character change.

This vile act compounds over time to cause a significant personality change in the victims: victims who used to be calm, fun-loving and the best of themselves are now depressed as a result of the mental abuse.

Gaslighting causes depression in victims after a while, as the constant letting down, blame-shifting, dissonance, and mental manipulation takes its toll on them.

The effects of gaslighting don't come all at once in victims; these effects occur in stages and victims will go through three steps when they suffer in the hands of a gaslighting narcissist: disbelief, defense, and depression. When depression sets it, the victim discards their own reality, and the narcissist wins.

Stage One: Disbelief.

Disbelief is the first reaction of the victim towards gaslighting behavior. They can't figure out what is happening and why the narcissist suddenly changes attitude towards them. Of course, the narcissists want this because, along the way, they know the victim will submit to their wishes, and they will control the victim's reality.

At first, the narcissist presented a different version of themselves to the victim. In the eyes of the victim, a narcissist is a person full of love, and they will find it hard to believe that a person that has once shown love to them is now something else.

This first stage is a state of total unawareness on the part of the victim. The victim is not aware of the gaslighting that is employed by the narcissist. All that they see is that the narcissist who once supported them and shown love to them is now very critical of them and any attempt to discuss the reason for the change of attitude is blocked or diverted into something not relevant to the reason why their attitude changed or in worse cases the attempt to discuss is met with silence.

At this stage, love-bombing stops and nitpicking starts: the victims are shocked about the narcissist's radical change of behavior. One minute, the narcissist was the perfect person, and now the narcissist is a shadow of their former selves.

The victim will still try to make sense of everything at this stage and might attribute the sudden change of behavior to another event in the life of the narcissist.

After a while, the narcissist might seem to be healthy and okay again in the eyes of the victim, but this is just temporary as the narcissists will come back powerfully with more force and their bad behavior will now become a never-ending cycle.

This is also the stage where the narcissist starts to create confusion in the victim's mind with their actions and words. Later on at this stage, the victim begins to become dependent on the narcissist for a sense of reality.

Stage two: Defense.

At this stage, the victim still has a grip on the part of their self to fight and defend themselves against the gaslighting manipulation. The narcissist at this point is gaslighting with covert threats, triangulation, and name-calling.

The narcissist is trying hard to make the victim think they are insane at this point, but a part of the victim is working hard to believe this while another part has accepted the fact that the victim is crazy.

This is the stage where the tactics of gaslighting are beginning to work, but the victim still has control over a little part of their mind. At this stage, gaslighting has worn out a part of the victim's mind; the victim begins to mentally weaken and starts to give in.

In any case, the narcissist's gaslighting is starting to do what it is expected to do, that is, to startle the victim, by creating self-doubt and guilt in them. This emotional harm causes the victim, after some time, to lose their sense of the real world, and their sense of self. They become lost and incapable of trusting in their own memory. The victim may start to feel shame and after a while, the victim will feel they are in great danger.

Psychologists believe that nature has built-in coping mechanisms from birth for when we feel we are about to be destroyed.

One of these coping mechanisms is explained as "Stockholm Syndrome" where the victim adapts to the traumatic situation by unconsciously reverting to childhood patterns of behavior, and bonds with their abuser as they did with their mother in their childhood when they feel threatened.

Another coping mechanism is "Cognitive Dissonance" where the victim seeks to rationalize the narcissist's behavior.

To defend themselves, victims do two things to cope with the gaslighting:

They rationalize the behavior of the abusive narcissist, and as such, they fall into a state of cognitive dissonance. This is a state of discomfort that occurs when a person holds contradictory ideas or beliefs in their minds at the same time. (*See Chapter Two*)

They revert to childhood behaviors as a defense against the narcissist's gaslighting. By going into this regressive mode, they begin to bond with the narcissist as they did with their mothers when they were babies. This is done unconsciously out of fear of the narcissist.

Stage three: Depression.

At this stage, gaslighting has taken its full effect, and the victim has now become a shadow of their former selves. They begin to think they can't make decisions anymore, they can't deal with reality any longer, and they withdraw into depression.

By this stage, the victim can barely recognize themselves, and they are rapidly turning into a shadow of their previous selves, living inside a war region where they are controlled physically and battered emotionally. The victim starts to avoid people, places, or thoughts and develop a lack of interest in activities that give them happiness and joy. They also begin to relive past experiences.

At this point, they begin to have difficulty concentrating on their tasks, and they feel hopeless.

They start to feel that they can't do anything right anymore, they don't think that they can trust their own mind and they escape into depression.

Many victims also go on to experience Post Traumatic Stress Disorder (PTSD). The symptoms of PTSD fall into three classes:

1. Reliving the past: (Flashbacks, bad dreams, and nervousness)

2. Avoidance: (Avoiding people, places, and a general lack of interest)

3. Arousals: (Hyper-vigilance, insomnia, frequent outbursts of anger)

Gaslighting can have disastrous impacts on a victim's mental wellbeing. The process of gaslighting is frequently slow, wearing down the victim's confidence and self-esteem gradually to a point where they may come to accept that they deserve the maltreatment or a point where the victim starts to question all that they hear, feel, and remember.

Gaslighting can likewise influence the victim's social life. The narcissist may control them into cutting ties with loved ones.

The survivors of gaslighting may struggle to trust others as they are always on the alert for further manipulation. They refuse to be vulnerable in future relationships. This refusal might cause problems again in future relationships.

Apart from refusing to show vulnerabilities, the survivors of gaslighting may also seek validation desperately in future relationships. They might put up with bad behaviors, and this may put them at risk of further narcissistic abuse.

The effects of gaslighting even continue after the victim has escaped the abusive relationship, as the impact of gaslighting might persist. The victim may still doubt their perceptions and have trouble making simple decisions. Victims are also less likely to voice what they truly feel, knowing that they are likely to be invalidated by others.

Chapter 6 – Top Ten Signs You are Being Manipulated with Gaslighting

If you have ever had a friend, family or co worker who was a narcissist, chances are you have been a victim of gaslighting, or maybe some effects on gaslighting mentioned earlier on resonate with you, or you know someone in your life who is always nitpicking and making covert threats. Whatever the case might be, you can associate someone with how gaslighting operates, and you need to validate if what you are feeling is true or not.

We looked into the common tactics used by gaslighting narcissists in chapter four, and we saw the effects gaslighting has on a victim in the last chapter. These effects don't happen all at once, but they take place over time in a gradual process.

One disturbing aspect of gaslighting is that everybody at risk, as truth be told, gaslighting is a strategy regularly used by cult leaders and tyrants. So, gaslighting is not only a prominent feature in personal relationships: we can experience gaslighting in everyday life without even realizing it.

Lamentably, gaslighting as a tactic for abuse can be used by the individuals who mean much to you, meaning it might be challenging to realize this fact because of the deliberate slow way in which it is being used as a tool for manipulation.

It's difficult to perceive this kind of abuse because, in addition to lying and bad behavior, the manipulator may be unbelievably charming.

So right now, you might be second-guessing trusted people in your life, and you might think all these signs are wrong. You might not know that you are in an abusive relationship.

It is now over to you as my reader to take a few minutes of your time to re-evaluate your life and see if any of these top ten signs hold true for you (or for anyone that you know). These signs are the most common signs of being manipulated with gaslighting by a victim; examine your relationships and see where any of these signs hold true:

1. Your vulnerabilities are used against you.

Have you ever shared your fears or vulnerabilities with anyone, and the person comes back later to poke at your weaknesses?

Narcissists are charming people who will listen to every word you say not because they are great listeners, but because they believe they can use your words against you come later, so they keep what you say about yourself in a mental file so that they can use it later.

Have you ever told someone a feature about yourself or a particular weakness of yours that you feel a bit insecure about? Features like your weight or your height, and discovered that the person pokes at that specific feature or weakness later? That is a sign of gaslighting, and chances are the person is a narcissist.

In addition to using your vulnerabilities against you, individuals who use gaslighting on you will use your loved ones or the activities you like to do against you. On the off chance that you cherish a particular activity, they will discover issues with it.

If you have kids you hold dear and cherish, the narcissist may lead you to believe you ought to never have had them. This abusive strategy makes the victim question themselves as well as the people they love and the activities they cherish.

So, if there is anyone you can think of right now that is always making reference to your weaknesses when you talk or when you argue, take a step back and see how often they do it and also, the situations where they talk about your vulnerabilities.

2. You question your mind.

Narcissists are known for their truth-bending abilities, and when they make promises and break them later on, they seek to evade responsibility for the broken promise.

Apart from promises, narcissists can also twist facts to fit their manipulative purposes, and when confronted for an evil deed, they can turn everything around and put it on the person that faces them.

In your relationships, examine the various scenarios where someone has let you down with a promise or does something to gain your attention and later on says they didn't make a promise, or they didn't perform that specific action. Is this trend repeating itself often? Does it happen day to day?

When you start to question your own perceptions after an interaction with a person you should watch out: a person says "A," and hearing this correctly, you later on mention "A" in a conversation with them, and the next thing is "I never said A, are you sure you are okay?"

Coupled with evading responsibility and lying, a narcissist will usually add a phrase that makes you question your mind or think you are going crazy.

When you ask a person about a promise or a past action or the words they said to you a while ago, and they turn it back on you, swearing not to understand you or saying you are too forgetful, you can begin to question yourself. Watch out, the narcissist is gaslighting you.

3. You are labeled as "paranoid", "too sensitive" or "hormonal."

A narcissist will shirk responsibility for their actions, and they will try to make you feel you are the wrong person in the relationship rather than their words and actions.

Is anyone in your life right now labeling you as "paranoid" or "too sensitive" or "hormonal," when you confront them for wrongdoing or when you try to correct them about a thing they have done wrong? Take a step back and examine your encounters with the person. You have never felt like you were excessively touchy in this past, but now in your relationship with someone, you are always being informed that you are sensitive and it's a big issue, and you begin to think about whether it is valid, which it's most certainly not.

Notice how someone says these words when you confront them about things they ought to do, or when you react to their wrongdoings.

The narcissist's actions will hurt you, yet you believe you can't utter a word since you would be called "too sensitive", "paranoid' or "hormonal."

4. You doubt your own beliefs and perception

This is perhaps the biggest red flag. You saw something, and you were clear in your mind you saw that thing, but while you were talking to that person in your life, you were made to believe that you didn't see what you thought you saw. There is a big chance you are falling victim to gaslighting by a narcissist.

Maybe in your relationship, your spouse says words like, "You don't know what a healthy relationship looks like." So, you regularly question your very own judgment and feel that your partner is more intelligent than you are.

Not only do you now doubt yourself, you additionally experience difficulty settling on your own choices because you think your choices are not healthy or wrong. You accept that whatever decision is made for you by your partner regardless of whether it is what you think is right for you or wrong.

5. You are always trying to keep the peace

Concealed threats, and aggression in language can be employed by a narcissist to cause fear and mental discomfort in victims.

Examine the recent course of events in your life. Do you find yourself always trying to keep the peace in a particular work or personal relationship? Or someone silently threatens you, and you are always trying to make peace. If you find yourself trying to keep peace in your relationships by doing what you don't want to do just because of fear of the other person, chances are you are with a gaslighting narcissist.

6. You stop trying to be heard

Relationships are for sharing and caring, and when you observe someone is ignoring you when you talk about your problems or feelings rather than listening and empathizing with you but will always want to talk to you about their own issues.

Altogether, you have stopped trying to communicate and

express how you truly feel to someone you are in a relationship with. It may be your spouse, boyfriend or girlfriend or even your co-worker or boss.

Step back and observe your relationships. Have you been trying to stop communicating your feelings to this other person? Then, you might be dealing with a narcissist.

7. You start thinking maybe you are the crazy one

Narcissists are famous for their selective memories, and they will deny that they ever said anything to hurt you when they are confronted with their words, finding a way to turn it back on you and make you think you heard them wrong.

When you find yourself thinking maybe you really are the crazy one in your relationships that's another red flag right there.

Are you involved with anyone who regularly makes you feel you are the crazy one, yet it is the other person always calling names, getting angry, and stepping on toes? The person might be a narcissist.

The narcissist will know when you are already questioning your sanity. The narcissist also knows that you would turn to them to seek clarity, along the line, when they call you insane, as you trust their judgment.

Furthermore, the narcissist may also tell other people that you are insane so that in any event you approach these people for help, they won't believe you, as the narcissist had already said you would seek help and you shouldn't be taken seriously.

8. You always believe you owe someone an apology.

Is there anyone in your life right now you are always saying sorry to, even when you never did anything wrong?

You should understand that a gaslighting narcissist is a master manipulator who will continuously guilt trip you by playing the victim who is giving everything up for you.

One of the most common indications of being a casualty of gaslighting is winding up as often as possible saying "I'm sorry", when there is nothing to be sorry about.

If your default reaction to anything is to apologize, this is a warning that you don't have a sense of speaking your own mind.

9. You are depressed and anxious.

A gaslighting narcissist will create an environment that will eventually drain the victim of emotions over time. A narcissist wears down a victim to a point where the victim feels hopeless, and the roller coaster of emotions the narcissist makes the victim go through makes the victim feel disoriented and anxious. Thanks to all the references about their memories, he or she may become incredibly depressed and anxious.

Is there anyone in your life whose thought takes away the joy you feel in an instant?

A narcissist will continuously use gaslighting on a victim. A lie here, a rude remark there, crazy-calling and then it goes down for the victim from there.

Indeed, even the most mindful individuals can be gradually sucked into mental manipulation because of the insidious manner of gaslighting.

People who are victims of gaslighting often feel like they can't speak freely in the presence of the narcissist without being criticized.

They feel tense and restless as they anticipate the narcissist to count their words as nothing or criticize them. Then again, they feel increasingly sure and free when they are far from the narcissist.

Being in this kind of relationship will eventually deplete the victim of vitality since they will invest so much energy considering what they ought to do or say next that won't be scrutinized.

Do you feel unhappy due to your relationship with a person in your life?

While it is normal to have misunderstandings and miscommunications, when you observe it is becoming a regular thing with someone in your life, and it is making you sad, check yourself for depression. If you truly feel anxious about this person, then you might be a victim of gaslighting.

The problem, of course, is the gaslighting narcissist in your life.

10. You think you are actually manipulated with gaslighting

Funny how you have gone through these signs to discover one of them holds true for one of the relationships in your life right now.

When you actually think you are being manipulated by

someone mental, a part of your mind that is still rational and healthy will actually send thoughts about a particular person in your life that is playing with your mind.

Our intuition works to help us as humans, and when you have a deep gut feeling about someone, then it is time to take a step back and see how you might have been a victim of gaslighting.

If there is any part of you having suspicions right now, then be sure that one of these signs or more is visible in your relationship with the "suspected" narcissist.

The gaslighting narcissist is less likely to put a stop to it right now, so take some time to confirm your suspicions.

The fact that you are suspicious means the rational part of your brain is still functioning and can pick up on cues of manipulation from your environment.

Did any of these signs seem to be familiar with you?

It is pertinent to note that there are other signs of manipulation apart from these ten signs. However, these top ten signs happen to be the most common signs of being manipulated by gaslighting narcissists. More examples will be presented in the next chapter.

In the next chapter, we will be examining the common

phrases narcissists say when they are gaslighting victims, and you will get to see the ugly reasons why they say what they say and do what they do. These phrases are also signs that show you how gaslighting narcissists wear their victims down with words.

Chapter 7 – 80 Things Narcissists Say During Gaslighting.

A t first, it may be hard to detect if a narcissist is trying to have their way with you because they might be hiding the fact that they are gaslighting you with their words.

The first step to taking back control of your emotions is to be aware of the words narcissists say during gaslighting.

There are ways to detect gaslighting in words, and in this chapter, we will see the words a narcissist uses to make you think you are crazy. If the signs of gaslighting in the previous chapter are not enough to pin down the narcissistic abuse, then maybe the phrases narcissists use will shed more light on the picture.

This collection of manipulative phrases are pointers to gaslighting, and if you observe that anyone uses more than ten of these phrases when they address you, then you can be certain that you are a victim of gaslighting.

The underlying reasons for the use of these phrases are also presented, which will aid your understanding of the roots of these words and make you see why narcissists carefully select them when they are trying to manipulate a victim into submission to their own will.

The 80 things narcissists say during gaslighting (in no particular order of importance) arc;

1. *"You are always making up this stuff in your head."*

2. *"You should get tested for paranoia."*

3. *"You are crazy, you are a freak, you are mad."*

4. *"Everyone in this town thinks you are bipolar."*

5. *"I never said that you are crazy."*

6. *"I never did that, you're crazy."*

7. *"You are delusional."*

8. *"You just listen to yourself; you're losing it."*

9. *"Everyone agrees with me — You are the crazy one."*

The statements on the previous page are attempts to make you think you didn't see the things you thought you saw or heard the things you thought you heard. They are meant to make you start doubting your senses.

Since the narcissist's goal is to make you dismiss your perceptions, after some time has passed, you may begin to address yourself and trust a portion of the narcissist's allegations about you.

You may even start to dismiss your own characteristics and qualities and make statements like, "I think I'm losing it." That is the goal of the narcissist, as once you believe you are crazy or delusional, you start to rely on the narcissist for your sanity.

You can see the tactical ways gaslighting narcissists operate with these words to make you think you are crazy. Can you see shaming and triangulation in these words?

Moving on:

10. *"You're so childish or immature. You need to learn to communicate better."*

11. *"Why are you getting upset over something little, get over it, I'm late, I was supposed to be here at 12.00pm, but I'm here now (2:30 p.m.) "*

12. *"I never do things wrong. You do"*

13. *"You treat me like a piece of shit, and you said you are not on drugs."*

14. *"You started it."*

15. *"Why are you so defensive?"*

16. *"If you didn't piss me off, I wouldn't have to say mean things to you."*

17. *"I'm not saying you need to be different, I'm not trying to change anybody. You are."*

18. *"It's always something with you."*

19. *"You have always got a problem."* Or *"you are a big problem."*

20. *"I don't answer your texts because you bother me with your stupidity."*

21. *"No wonder your son isn't good at math; you are also good for nothing."*

22. *"You are always looking for something to grip at all the time."*

These phrases are used to make you think you are responsible for the narcissist's actions when narcissists make mistakes, as they look for a scapegoat instead of taking responsibility. You should note how everything always seems to be your fault when it is clear that you are never capable of making someone do what they have decided not to do in the first place.

Habitually, a narcissist is always in attack mode, and they seldom, if at any time, own up to their very own imperfections or inadequacies. On the off chance that they are criticized or held responsible for something, they rush to accuse others while excusing their behavior.

Even when reality appears perfectly clear to you, a narcissist still won't concede that they are not right.

23. *"I'm much smarter than you, dumbass!"*

24. *"I'm from a bloodline of smart men. I'm smarter than average people like you."*

25. *"Someone told me that they had the best time ever because I was there."*

26. *"I'm the best thing that has ever happened to you."*

27. *"I have a friend; he is the CEO of (a company) who owns whatever. I have lots of friends. You are the loser who stays home all the time with no friends."*

28. *"I was rich beyond belief back in California, and I knew all the movie stars you know because I grew up with them, and I never had to worry about being broke all the time."*

29. *"My job is more important. You just have projects. It's just busywork. That's no job."*

30. *"I know exactly what you are thinking."*

31. *"You're a piece of shit.*

32. *Don't worry about it. Shut up you are such a fool. You worry about everything. I've done this before."* (If you try to let them know that they are going to get in some kind of trouble)

33. *"It's my way or the highway, bitch."*

34. *"Somebody has to earn a living." "I am working my ass off, but nobody around here seems to care."*

Because narcissists put themselves on a pedestal and can't dole out praise to you when you do something splendid, they will always be in a silent competition with you: they are smarter, they have more friends, they are the hard-working ones. They feel threatened when you shine for your own efforts and will always find a way to undermine you and make you feel smaller compared to them.

Consider the things you have done that deserve praise. Are they always things that benefit a particular person in your life? Were you lavished with praise by that person in your life?

Provided that this is true, this is simply one more variety of oppressive gaslighting since you don't get applauded for the things that you truly deserve to be praised for.

35. *"You are too stupid, no one will ever like you."*

36. *"You're too fat."*

37. *"You're too sensitive."*

38. *"Nobody likes you."*

39. *"You never listen."*

40. *"You're just over-sensitive." "Stop being so sensitive."*

41. *"No one will ever love you the way I do." "You will never find anyone as good as I am."*

These phrases are said to hurt your feelings, and once the narcissist feels a part of you gets sensitive or reacts to these phrases, they continue to hurt you until your self-esteem falls. What the narcissists fail to realize is the fact that no single being is perfect, but they are too self-absorbed to realize this, and in their own eyes, they are the perfect ones.

Did you observe "name-calling" as discussed in Chapter Four in these words?

42. *"If you tell them about what I said, I will make your life miserable and hurt you."*

43. *"Go ahead, tell your friends and family about me. Just know if you do, I will make your life a living hell."*

44. *"Everyone thinks I'm a pretty nice guy, it's a shame you don't."*

45. *"No wonder (name) and (name) has a problem with you." "You are too selfish."*

46. *"I don't give a crap about our kids."*

47. *"Knock yourself out. Make a fool of yourself."*

48. *"You'll never find anyone to put up with you like I do."*

49. *"You will never live in a house as nice as this one. You will end up living on the streets."*

Gaslighting narcissists use threats in covert ways as when they know a few of your fears they turn them against you and use them as a tool to manipulate you into doing their bidding.

At times, they use people against you, as the narcissists know who will defend them no matter what they do and the people who won't protect them, and some other times they try to make you feel that people don't like you.

Know for sure that when narcissists try to play you against people, they do it so that you feel there is no one to trust. They isolate you by making you question the people you can trust; they are separating you because it gives them the authority over you that they want.

Some other phrases gaslighting narcissists use are:

50. "What do you get out of being moody all the time?"

51. "I used to think you were a great person."

52. "I'm not arguing with you, I'm just discussing."

53. "I don't have time for your games."

54. "Just try, you'll lose, loser!"

55. "You like being a victim. That is why I stay away from you."

56. "You just sit around and play on the computer all day."

57. "I'm going to stay away from you, you put me down."

58. "If I want to feel crazy, I will come to you. You suck!"

59. "No one will ever love you the way I do." "Why do you have to get all hurt over stuff?"

60. "I know how to do, I know why you do, I know how you do." "I know the answers, and you have to listen to me."

61. "You just want to bring up things from the past."

62. "You should know this is not a good time to talk."

63. "You can never do anything without me!" then after a while, "I never said that you're crazy."

64. "You have no friends."

65. "I'm not trying to control, you're thinking about your ex, and you're taking it out on me."

66. "I am the only one who really loves you."

67. "Watch what I do next ... "

68. " You can't take a joke. Can you?"

69. "I am going to pay you back on Friday." (And of course, they never do).

70. "You had better take that look off your face, or I will do it for you."

71. "Stop telling people stuff about me.

72. "You'll never find another man as good as me."

73. "Women were born to serve men."

74. "You are here to serve me; men are here to serve women."

75. "I can say anything I want to you because I own you."

"I criticize you because I love you."

76. *"Don't nag me." "Why are you upset? I was just kidding."*

77. *"Anger, what anger? So I'm not allowed to get angry?"*

78. *"I'll kill them and you."*

79. *"Get over it." "Grow up."*

80. *"Don't you think you're over-reacting?"*

A person outside the scenarios where these phrases are used would never know they are used by a gaslighting narcissist to achieve certain ends, as it takes a deeper reflection on what is happening around where these words are used to catch a glimpse of the subtle act of gaslighting.

These eighty phrases are a collection of common gaslighting phrases. The reason why you should pay attention to them is to create real awareness, so you realize the issues in your personal relationships.

Rather than blame yourself that the relationship turned out to be this bad, you can set a goal to improve your circumstances. Be thoughtful and know that you truly deserve better. Deciding to move forward will give you the inner strength to improve your situation.

If you observe that someone you relate with regularly uses these phrases when they talk to you, then its time you seize control of your sanity back. You can learn how to disarm the narcissist and win back the control for your mind.

Chapter 8 - Crush Gaslighting | Six Empowering Ways to Disarm a Narcissist and Take Control

The preceding chapter showed some phrases narcissists use in gaslighting. You are genuinely convinced that something is wrong somewhere in one of your relationships, as some of the signs presented in this book so far point to the fact that you are a victim of gaslighting, and now you want to take control of your thoughts back.

While a significant number of people can experience the world around them and figure out how to manage the good and bad times that are parts of life, narcissists are prone to keeping their environment very well controlled. Whatever they can't control, they blame people around them for.

The need for control is what makes narcissists challenging to work and relate with. Regardless of the fact that you have a decent argument or a solution to a problem, the narcissist will still use their collection of ammunition to bring others down and make them take the blame.

Your interaction with the gaslighting narcissist might have caused you considerable amounts of stress and pressure. The narcissist's need for power and control will always make them develop creative ways of getting what they want. In the end, you will even end up taking all the blame for every bad thing that has happened.

The awareness of the fact that you have been a victim of gaslighting goes a long way in restoring you to a healthy state. It is no easy feat because at this point, you might have been crippled emotionally, and it will take some efforts to disarm a narcissist and seize control for the sake of your sanity.

However, it is possible to overcome emotional abuse and mental manipulation by learning the empowering ways with which you can disarm a narcissist. To take the control from the narcissist, you have to take the focus off the pain you feel and realize that this pain is a typical sign of emotional abuse. You need to focus on how to disarm the narcissist so that you can take back full control for your thoughts.

These are the six ways you can empower yourself to disarm the narcissist:

1. **Disengage from the situation.**

The first way to disarm a narcissist is to take your energy back. You allow yourself to be emotionally drained when you get yourself caught up in the drama with a narcissist.

You have realized that you are being manipulated with gaslighting, so don't allow any more drama with the narcissist: stop arguing with them, don't try to explain yourself, don't get caught in their web of lies, detach yourself.

Gaslighting narcissists love to argue and fight with words, as they know how to make you react with their words, and they know when they push you to the point where you will try to protect yourself verbally. Keeping your calm will throw the narcissist off balance, and nothing will infuriate them more than you trying to keep your composure.

Keeping your cool will leave the narcissist no choice but to walk away or change their behavior.

When you withdraw your attention, they stop in their tracks to examine their tactics and might even come back stronger, but as long as you don't give in, you frustrate their efforts, and they will start keeping their distance.

However, doing this works fine for the gaslighting narcissist who is in most cases often less toxic than psychopaths and sociopaths who might take on the fact that you are refusing to give in to drama to the level of physical abuse.

Don't fall for the temptation of coming down to their level.

2. Control your emotions.

Similar to disengaging from the situations where you feel the narcissist is saying gaslighting phrases to mess with your head, controlling your emotions when they use hurtful words is another way to disarm the narcissist.

Keep your cool. Displaying an emotion will only make the narcissist come back stronger in the bad behavior, as they will get encouragement from the fact that you are now angry and continue to behave in the same way with you.

Along with disengaging the narcissist, control your own emotions so as not to react when they say words that might make you angry.

The narcissist's power wanes when you control yourself.

3. Stop saying, "I am sorry."

Due to the fear of being criticized or being hurt with abusive words, you must have been repeating this statement unconsciously in your relationship with the narcissist.

Not saying sorry is another way to disarm the narcissist. You must have found yourself apologizing for how the narcissist feels and how you feel; you have been apologizing for the things you do and the things you didn't do, and you have been apologizing for everything including the things that went wrong through no fault of yours.

Stop apologizing. By always apologizing, you are feeding that part of a narcissist where they see themselves as perfect, and you are only making them stronger.

You are not in any way responsible for the narcissist's emotions, so stop taking responsibility for how they feel. Stop, as you will always be the one reinforcing their negative behaviors.

4. Put your needs first.

This is about asserting yourself. Too often you have been putting the needs of the narcissist over your own needs. You should realize that taking care of yourself means doing the things you love to do and loving yourself doesn't imply that you are selfish.

You have also unconsciously been willing your power away to the narcissist by taking care of their needs first. This comes out of the teachings of being selfless we all had as kids: you were taught that being selfless was good.

When these patterns continue into adulthood and you push yourself to the limits, you might start to let go of your own needs to take care of others.

If you take care of yourself first there is a lesser chance of you being taken advantage of by the narcissist. Know your needs and seek to fulfill them first.

The mind-destroying effects of gaslighting can make you think you deserve the bad things that happened to you. You can blame yourself for being such a bad person.

You don't need to attempt to do all things at once. Instead, start with little goals that can improve your situation now that you are aware of your case. Be thoughtful of yourself and realize that you merit love regardless of how you might feel.

5. Set Clear Boundaries.

Putting in place the proper boundaries to protect means you take more of a confrontational approach, as you let the narcissist know what you are willing to take and what you are not.

Setting boundaries doesn't always seem easy to learn, but it can be learned as a skill with constant practice.

To start setting clear boundaries for yourself:

1. You need to know the things you are not comfortable with in relationships. Anything that makes you feel discomfort, anger, or resentment with an individual may be because your limits have been crossed by that individual. A list of things you are not comfortable with will change over time, and you need to re-assess yourself regularly.

2. After knowing the things that make you uncomfortable, it is right for you to follow through on them, as being assertive is the way you let others become aware that they are crossing your boundaries. Be direct in your approach, and when the other person keeps violating your clearly stated boundary then you can tell them they are disrespecting you and ignore them from that point on.

An excellent way to set a boundary with the narcissist is to put it in writing and keep a copy pasted where the narcissist will always see it. Also, put into writing the consequences of what will happen when the narcissist violates your boundaries.

You are setting clear boundaries to protect yourself from further abuse.

6. Re-Build Your Sense of Identity.

Emotional abuse by a narcissist can make you lose your sense of self and your self-worth. Rebuilding means you have to let go of the old self that was manipulated and abused and start to invest in a brand new you.

Wake up every morning and visualize your future self for a set-aside number of minutes. Hold on to this future self as you proceed with your daily activities and believe you can truly be that better version of yourself.

It means to quit holding the narcissist responsible for your worth, whoever they might be, so you become reliant on yourself for your own happiness.

You will make it your mission to self-actualize your development past the recent abuse and pick up the pieces of yourself that you were forced to give away by looking up to the narcissist to grant you love, approval, and security.

These six ways are to empower you to take back full control of your life. Some of these ways help in personal and work relationships while others are ways to disarm the narcissists in personal relationships.

In most cases, almost everyone has either worked for a narcissistic boss or been exposed to one in some working situations, and not only bosses alone can be narcissists at work co-workers, and subordinates can be too.

Most times, it's an unforgettable encounter to associate with narcissists at work as they are people who are so outrageously self-absorbed, conceited and self-obsessed that they are quick to take praise for the efforts of others and also quick to lay the blame on others when things go wrong. Narcissistic co-workers and subordinates at work will only work hard when they know someone else is watching.

A narcissistic boss, on the other hand, invests a great measure of their energy contemplating accomplishing significant impact, and achievement. Therefore, they have a propensity to lie and overstate reality to feel vainglorious. A narcissistic boss will never think they're the problem. A narcissistic boss will always have a scapegoat to blame when something goes wrong.

Since your job is essential, it is best you know how to handle narcissists at work if you can't attempt to change your job. By understanding the best way to react to things at work, you will be able to protect yourself from abuse. Here are the ways you can empower yourself at work to shield yourself from narcissistic conduct:

7. Know that narcissists can never change.

To adapt to a working environment where there are narcissistic co-workers or bosses, you need to accept the fact that narcissists don't change easily. The chances are high that they're never going to change, and they're never going to be anything but difficult to work with. This awareness will go a long way in protecting you when you hear gaslighting phrases.

Everybody can change in the event that they need to. However, one of the severe issues with narcissists is that since they never accept they have an issue, they have no inspiration to change.

Be that as it may, narcissists represent a fascinating problem. One of the signs of narcissism is a failure to be self-aware, and this unawareness of themselves leads to their belief in the fact that nothing is wrong with them and they are never the problem in any relationship.

Narcissists are also amazingly self-absorbed and will, in general, overestimate their achievements. They have a hard time taking criticism and assume no liability for their own emotions or actions, and often times resort to anger when they don't get what they want.

8. Manage your thoughts and actions with emotional intelligence

Narcissists at work will always like to get under your skin. They get a mental high when they shame you, embarrass you, disgrace you or call you out and when you react without thinking first, they feel they have power over you. The most terrible thing you can do with a narcissist is to get in a war of words with them. Instead, figure out how to react in a way that keeps you responsible for choices and decisions.

Emotional intelligence is the ability to manage one's emotions very well. Emotional intelligence is about self-awareness, self-control, empathy, and working as a team with others. These are parts of emotional intelligence that you must learn how to practice from day to day at work, to effectively manage your own reactions until you can get away from the reach of the narcissist.

Self-awareness is all about knowing your triggers and your emotions, along with your strengths and weaknesses. Self-control means you can manage your own emotions and strive to achieve balance in what you do. Empathy doesn't necessarily mean agreeing with your co-workers, subordinates, or bosses, but it means you see their thoughts and emotions for what it is and understand and appreciate them.

Working as a team means you find common ground with those around you (it is often hard to find common ground with the narcissist).

 On the off chance that you feel caught in a web of a fight with a narcissist, step away, and control yourself, and remember that the narcissist's behavior and words are a reflection of who they are

9. Set Clear Boundaries at Work too

Set clear limits. Set a firm limit wherever you need one and stick to it. Setting boundaries is totally healthy as it helps you put restrictions on how others can behave to you. It is being assertive and standing up for yourself when you need to.

Set boundaries for what you will accept and what you won't starting from your first day at the job.

Keep in mind, limits aren't intended to control others, they are just guidelines for others to know and to realize what is and isn't worthy when it comes to you.

10. Double-check everything.

Double-check everything. A narcissist will consistently depict themselves as an unfortunate casualty who is guiltless in all aspects, and at any point when reality upsets them (which is regularly) they're brisk to trade reality for lies and misleading statements.

Whether you have a narcissistic boss or co-worker or subordinate at work, be prepared to do a ton of fact checking.

11. Stay Focused on What is Important

Remain concentrated on what's significant. You have to hold on to what your purpose at being in a particular job is for when things get messy with your boss or co-workers.

Working with a narcissist boss implies a steady pull to play by their rules and principles as everything revolves around them, with no responsibility or accountability when things turn out badly. It's difficult to not feel angry, frustrated and disappointed when you work around these personalities and when things are not going as expected. That is the point at which you need to make a step back and reconnect with your motivation for being at work.

12. Refuse to Encourage Bad Behavior

A narcissistic boss will always have a steady need to be respected by others. Know a narcissist's awful conduct comes from their insecurities, and that the more bad behavior they show, the more insecure they are. So, refuse to feed their egos by promoting their bad behaviors because if you do, they will only get worse.

The same holds for your co-workers and subordinates. Try not to engage the individuals who don't merit it. Do not encourage bad behaviors.

Simply carry out your responsibilities with respect and integrity. When you do, you'll be seen as one of the normal ones at work.

It might be easy to think that you can just drop the narcissist and move on with your life, but sometimes it is far easier said than done. You need to know how to disarm a narcissist to make living and working with them tolerable.

It is essential you know that you can't change a narcissist. The best you can do is to protect yourself from abuse and take control of your own life.

Chapter 9 – Gaslighting Repellent | How to Shut Down a Narcissist

Narcissists don't process or experience feelings how healthy individuals do, and this is reflected in their damaging conduct. All things considered, you can't react to a narcissist in the way you may react to other individuals and anticipate a comparable result.

The narcissist sees their conduct as ordinary. They control, exploit, and carry around a misrepresented sense of self-importance that makes them genuinely believe that they are generally morally justified. Every other person is the issue. Due to this and many of their numerous character issues and psychological maladjustments, the narcissist leaves casualties of destroying maltreatment in their wake.

To shut down a narcissist, you have to see how they experience, process, and respond to emotions, and everybody in their environment.

A narcissist will poke at your vulnerabilities as they try to manipulate you, and therefore it is necessary to know and own your weaknesses before you can shut down a narcissist.

When a narcissist says something critical about a vulnerability of yours, it puts you into a mode of defense, you feel threatened, and you can't think through the solution to the problem at hand.

Entering defense mode, psychologists say comes from the need to protect ourselves when we face a threatening situation, as the rational part of the brain is totally shut in this mode, and only our survival matters.

In our relations with others, it is not often necessary to enter defense mode, but the narcissist is always self-absorbed as they seek to fulfill only their own needs always. Narcissists are always on defense mode and will attempt to put the people around them in this mode, which results in two people who are too occupied with protecting themselves instead of logically tackling a problem.

Now let's take a look at the common types of vulnerability themes. Here you will identify the ones the narcissist has been exploiting to make you think you are crazy:

Abandonment. This is a familiar feeling that the people in your life will not be there for you. You feel you can't count on your parents, your siblings, or people close to you for emotional support. It is a feeling of fear that the important people in your life will leave you.

Abandonment can be a form of anxiety, and the loss of people is a characteristic of life, whether it is the end of a relationship or passing on of a loved one.

Be that as it may, individuals with abandonment issues live in dread of losing people. They may likewise unintentionally do things that push individuals to leave so they're never surprised when people leave them.

A fear of abandonment isn't a recognized condition in mental health, per se. Instead, it's considered a type of fear and is treated as such. Some indicators of this kind of vulnerability are:

- You feel your parents won't be there when you need them.

- You feel your siblings or close friends won't be there for you.

- You continuously need assurance from friends and loved ones, and you urge them to make statements like "I will always be there for you."

Shame. This is a psychological feeling of inadequateness, that you are not good enough or inferior to others, that others won't love who you are and will always reject you.

Shame has to do with the negative feelings we have about

ourselves, which are triggered whenever we are disappointed or when we get tested by a challenging situation.

Shame is one of the most dominant feelings that we feel as humans. It can make us cut off social connections, fuel our addictions, and sink us into a pit of depression. It might even lead to suicide in some cases.

For many individuals, shame is a feeling they feel to a shifting degree consistently.

How do you recognize this kind of vulnerability?

- ➢ You are feeling insecure around others, you think you are too tall, too short, not intelligent enough, etc.

- ➢ Whenever you figure you've accomplished something incorrectly or you don't know something, you feel slightly awkward in social situations.

- ➢ You can't take constructive feedback and criticism, and you are always reacting.

- ➢ You fear others will hurt you if you get too close to them.

Pessimism. Is a general view that everything is wrong with you and with the world. When your outlook to the world we live in is negative, individuals who incline toward pessimism may likewise feel defenseless and accept that any moves made are probably not going to generate a positive result. Pessimism makes individuals believe themselves to be passive beings on the planet and to a great extent, will attribute any chance of accomplishment to factors that can't be controlled.

> ➢ You think life is always full of pain and disappointment.

> ➢ When the phone rings, you assume the caller will be a bill collector.

> ➢ You fail to recognize the positive aspects of life.

> ➢ You fear to make mistakes because of the catastrophic events that'd happen after your mistakes.

Self-Sacrifice is the belief that the needs of others should come at the expense of your own needs.

> ➢ You think that it is better to sacrifice your own needs, or desires for someone else.

> ➢ You like to prevent others from feeling pain to

avoid the guilt of being selfish.

If you have any of these vulnerabilities, it might be difficult for you to see things with a rational mind and from a logical point of view when you are in conflict with a narcissist. By taking into account your own vulnerabilities, you give the narcissist less power to control your emotions.

The narcissist's conduct is not the slightest bit your fault. Nobody has the right to be controlled, utilized, and abused. Despite this fact, the narcissist will regularly make you really believe that you are at fault, and you do deserve to be abused.

All things considered, it's vital to note that a relationship is a two-way road, like the biological example of a parasite and a host. The parasite can't work without its host. You will need to do some self-reflection to make sense of what you're getting from your relationship with the narcissist.

Sometimes, your physical home or family may be at stake. In different cases, the narcissist's attention on you may be, to some degree, soothing – regardless of how destructive this attention gets. Perhaps you like specific characteristics or have tender memories with the narcissist, or maybe in spite of everything you believe they can truly change.

You have to access whatever emotional vulnerabilities you

carry, assess them before pushing ahead so you can close down a narcissist for good.

Therefore, when a narcissist comes and pushes a button on any of your vulnerabilities, give yourself space to catch your breath and interrupt you going into defense mode, since you are now aware of your weaknesses.

You can gain control of your emotions with empowering thoughts or sayings like:

"I will take a moment to calm myself down so I can respond to this (event) rationally."

"I deserve to be listened to and respected, even if I feel bad this very minute, this (event) is not through any fault of mine."

If you have a personal relationship with the narcissist, phrases like these will help you:

"I suggest that we postpone this conversation until you have had a chance to calm down."

"It is clear that you are used to taking charge and having things go your way, but it's not okay for you to dismiss my opinions and feelings."

When you adjust your mindset instead of being defensive, you can respond assertively. In professional situations, you can say these phrases to help calm the situation:

"I'm ready to work this out with you, but I am not willing to be insulted by you."

"I would like to maintain a respectful working relationship with you, but I'm concerned with...."

"You are entitled to your opinion."

"We see things differently."

"I can see you that you feel very strongly about this."

"Let's talk when you are feeling calmer and ready to stop yelling."

However, it is by a wide margin the best answer to repelling a narcissist is the one that we should all acknowledge more frequently.

Narcissists don't have empathy for others, and put little effort into making people around them hopeless and miserable. In half a month to a couple of months, they can make everyone around them hopeless. Furthermore, narcissism is difficult to change. Thus, if at all possible, simply keep yourself away from the narcissist.

Don't for one moment think you are smarter than the narcissist. Just keep distance if you can.

Chapter 10 – Gaslighting Through Technology | How Narcissists Employ Smart Devices

New advances in technology have aided the production of new smart devices like connected thermostats, electronic keypad locks, audio players and security cameras, just to name a few, that can be operated remotely using smartphones. Technological companies make these smart products, and these products were designed to be operated remotely to help people remotely supervise their homes and control their devices when they are at work or on vacation.

There has been a rise in the number of people who call helplines for help after discovering that various smart devices around their homes are behaving in unusual ways. Smart devices were designed to make lives more comfortable and give humans more peace of mind, but they can be turned against humans when their control is placed in the hands of abusive individuals.

Placing the control of these smart home products in the hands of abusive individuals can be detrimental for many reasons, and one of these reasons is that the control of these products can give the abuser the power to turn technology against others.

117

Also, the idea of owning a smart home with interconnected smart devices is now being accepted by the millions over the world, and sooner or later, more products will be interconnected, which means that there will be an abundance of technology soon in our society that could be potentially used for abuse.

Smart home devices can be used by a gaslighting narcissist to make the victim question their sanity, because of the ease of control of these devices in most cases, as they were designed to be controlled remotely.

Of course, narcissists who engage in gaslighting are often brilliant people who are going to find a way of using these new technologies to manipulate people mentally and gain control over them.

A gaslighting narcissist can manipulate with smart electronic devices, and since they can be operated remotely, a narcissist can lock their victims out of the house, control house temperature, turn off lights, close windows and doors and use home security cameras to spy on victims.

These are just a few ways in which a narcissist might use technology to aid their mental manipulation and abuse. The gaslighting narcissist might turn the television on and off or mess with the thermostat and of course when they are confronted about what is happening, they can say the usual phrases they use in gaslighting:

"Why would I do that?"

"I didn't do that. Are you sure you are okay?"

It is good to examine the words and actions of people you are in relationships with, particularly when you think you're going crazy because your smart home lock no longer opens for you or the temperature in the house comes down to a freezing point or rises to sweltering heat, the television starts playing annoying content, or music randomly starts to play at high volumes at odd hours. Someone around you might be trying to use smart devices to make you think you are crazy.

On mobile smartphones, apps designed for monitoring children's phones can be installed on a partner's phone for spying on them without their consent, and in the same vein, keystroke tracking on a computer, or remote monitoring of the computer, can also be used to by a narcissist to play tricks with the victim.

As people who constantly seek attention and validation from others, the narcissist can use cellphones as a tool to keep people focused on them. Narcissists want to converse with you when they wish to and paying little heed to how sensible it is to call you at some points of your day, they will go ahead and call you. More than once, until you answer, if necessary.

In the case of calling your cellphone to no avail, they start sending you texts. When a narcissist starts to message you, they may already be angry at the fact that you weren't there when they needed to converse with you.

At the same time, a gaslighting narcissist will use technology such as a cell phone to manipulate. For example, a narcissist will intentionally avoid your calls or your texts to make you start wondering what they are up to. Also, they might answer you in one word when they pick up your call, just to put you off balance and instill doubts or fear in you.

In official scenarios, software packages like photoshop can be used in gaslighting. The narcissist will stop at nothing to undermine you at work and may photoshop to falsify bank exchange papers, official documents and so forth, and then you come into the office and start wondering how on earth you have acquired such papers. Even credit card charges can be falsified, and you will begin to wonder where you have made a particular purchase unknowingly.

Gadgets like webcams can also be used by a narcissist, as narcissists are control freaks and a webcam makes it easy for them to spy into victims' lives. Webcams can be employed to follow the routines and activities of every minute by the narcissist, which, in turn, will give them an unlimited supply of videos which they can play again and again to get pieces of information to use in controlling you.

Strategies for dealing with gaslighting through technology:

1. Choose a secure password for your phone, and other password enabled devices and change them in the event of a break-up or fight in a relationship. A narcissistic ex-spouse or lover can use this to collect information for manipulative purposes.

2. Contact your phone provider to help check your device for any spyware or tracking devices to check if there are no issues with your device and if your phone provider can't do something like this, it is advisable to get a new phone entirely and start afresh.

Remember that narcissists are very often intelligent people. Their goal is to cause victims to feel uncomfortable, and to make them feel out of control with their lives. In the years to come, technology will even make things easier for the narcissist, so if you ever find yourself in a position that makes you feel uncomfortable, do all you can to ensure you are safe.

Chapter 11 – How to deal with the Effects of Gaslighting

The most insidious thing about gaslighting is that it denies the victim of reality, telling them they didn't see what they just saw with their own eyes, or they didn't hear what they thought they heard by telling them their perceptions of what is right is wrong.

Countless people over the globe have fallen victims to this unique form of abuse at one point or the other in their lives and having survived the ordeal, they choose to share their experience with others, and by doing so, they disclose how they managed to cope with the awful situation.

Ariel Leve is a renowned survivor of narcissistic childhood abuse, and in her childhood memoir, she tells of how she grew up with a narcissistic mother and the horrible abuses she went through. She is just one of the countless people who have survived narcissistic abuse and manipulation.

In interviews and talks, she shares four strategies she used to deal with the abuse with others and we will further those strategies by adding plans from other survivors to throw light upon how to deal with gaslighting and help the victims cope with the situation.

1. Remaining Defiant.

Remaining defiant means holding on to your story of the abuse. It means trusting your own version of events and not allowing them to be altered on demand. A narcissist will try to bully you into accepting their own version of reality but trust your version of the real world.

Being defiant also means you realize what makes a difference to you, and you don't allow it to be adjusted or meddled with by anybody. It is tuning in to your own internal voice that knows better than anything said by another person.

You don't have to argue or contend with the narcissist — you just need to stand by your choices with absolute confidence.

Remaining defiant also makes you resilient in the face of abuse.

2. Accepting the fact that there will never be accountability on the part of a narcissist

There is no way the narcissist will ever take responsibility for their actions, as they don't know how to acknowledge their misdeeds as they are not people who can apply logic and reason to a situation.

You on your own part should keep a good record of events as they happen, for a narcissist will never acknowledge the fact that they are using gaslighting tactics to manipulate you.

If you speculate you are a victim of gaslighting, recording everything that has been said and done to you by the abuser is an excellent method to know who is truly right and what is truly right.

Writing things down, particularly exchanges that occur between you and the narcissist provides a solid defense for you when you are being manipulated to think against what is right.

Written proof of any faulty exchange is solid protection against anybody attempting to pull the wool over your eyes and will enable you to comprehend reality when you're being questioned.

3. Letting go of the wish for things to be different

Your hope for the narcissist to change can never prevail. Wishing for things to be changed is hoping that after a while, the narcissist will come to use reason and logic in dealing with you.

Also, after cycles of failed promises, a narcissist will still come around to promise that the bad things they do will never happen again. If you truly wish for things to be different, you'd see how the narcissist is manipulating you with the promises.

A gaslighting narcissist will always move the ground you stand on, and you have to stop wishing they would change their nature or events will turn out differently later. You have got to accept the situation and assess the ways you can seek to empower yourself.

4. Developing a healthy detachment

Detaching from the gaslighting situation doesn't mean total detachment from real life, it just recognizes the difference in the world of the narcissist and the real world.

A healthy detachment means you don't need the narcissist to validate what reality is for you, and it involves developing healthy coping mechanisms, and writing is one of the ways to do this.

Sure, some certain circumstances will make you remain in close association with a narcissist, but really, the best choice for you might be to abandon the relationship altogether. You can't change a narcissist, and if there is a chance that the gaslighting narcissist doesn't alter their injurious conduct, then leaving the relationship for your psychological and emotional wellbeing is your best choice.

Try not to let the narcissist persuade you that things will be extraordinary if you stay or that you are just overreacting to issues. Once again asking you to stay might be another pointer to gaslighting as a person who truly wants to change will recognize their wrongdoings and apologize for their bad behavior and will be willing to put efforts into making the relationship work.

5. Confiding in a Trusted Support System

You can always count on a trusted friend, a loved one or a professional if you suspect a narcissist is gaslighting you. By opening up to someone, you get to check and validate your reality.

Not only is opening up to a trusted person an added form of documentation, opening up to trusted people can help you understand what is happening to you better and also help you gain the courage to walk away.

Build up your own emotionally supportive network.

You need other individuals throughout life who can affirm your reality and self-worth. Gaslighting narcissists often try to isolate their victims to remain in charge.

Gaslighting narcissists might even go further into manipulating you to think they are the only people who care about you and understand you perfectly. Don't believe their lies. Spend time with loved ones. Check out your thoughts, feelings, and perceptions by talking to them.

Get professional help in the event that you need it. Victims of gaslighting frequently lose trust in their own thoughts and emotions and end up apprehensively double-checking themselves all the time.

Sometimes, you may sink into depression, and you will definitely need the help of a licensed professional to help you recover from the insidious effects of gaslighting.

6. Dismissing Self-blame

It is imperative to know that narcissists have psychological issues they are not willing to address and thus can project their wounds onto other people and become harmful and harsh to them. It is pertinent to note that how they treat you is an impression of how they feel about themselves.

The dismal truth is that your abuser may never acknowledge or concede what they were doing. For the most part since they don't believe they're doing anything incorrectly.

All you can do is recall that there's nothing you could have done any other way. Rational thinking doesn't work with a gaslighter.

You should not bear the responsibility. Comprehend that their wrong ways aren't your shortcoming.
While the reason for gaslighting is to wear you out, it's essential to remain as defiant and careful as you can.
When you truly understand what gaslighting is, you also get to know your options, and you're nearer to the enlightening reality of your circumstance so you can choose what's best for you.
The essence of these strategies is for you to realize that the narcissist eventually needs control of your life, and this is the reason why they seek to keep you away from making your life as autonomous and independent as could be expected under the circumstances.
Put the time into your own interests and friends. Be as dedicated to your own life as you are with your relationship.

Chapter 12 – Can Narcissists Trick Intelligent People?

G aslighting is a form of psychological manipulation used by the narcissist to make victims count on them for perceptions of the world. Narcissists are often intelligent people who use gaslighting to try to take control of their victim's thoughts and emotions.

Gaslighting is done in the subtlest of ways and so the signs are easy to miss. The way gaslighting is carried out is the reason why smart people can easily fall victim to this favorite weapon of the narcissist.

So why does gaslighting work so well on intelligent people?

Well, gaslighting works on the most intelligent people for several reasons:

1. **Intelligent people often possess the tendency to project their own morality, empathy, and conscience onto others.**

Most intelligent people have the tendency to project their qualities of empathy and good conscience onto others. They believe other people will act with the highest moral standards too.

They are emphatic people who feel other peoples' feelings strongly. They walk into the room and immediately spread good energy, and so their genuine feelings for others often lead them to the error of believing that everyone has true feelings for others too.

Intelligent people will assume the best about everyone, and this belief will mean they do not easily see that they are being manipulated.

2. Narcissists naturally gravitate to those who have the qualities they admire.

Too often, intelligent people attract narcissists not only because of their intelligence but also because of other qualities they may possess.

A wealthy, beautiful, emphatic and intelligent woman might, for example, be a "goal" for the narcissist since the narcissist is always about what they want: a successful and intelligent woman might look like an extra source of income to the narcissist.

The more successful an intelligent person is, the more they would look like objects to be captured by a narcissist, and it is natural for the narcissist to seek control of successful people so that they can have what they have.

3. Past trauma conditions intelligent people into associating love with abuse

This is also not only true for smart people, and also it doesn't apply to most smart people, but in some cases, victims of childhood traumas can carry their wounds into adulthood.

When the wounds of past hurts are not healed, the intelligent adult often tolerates abusive behavior and confuse it with love.

4. Human vulnerabilities have nothing to do with the rational mind.

Narcissists sense the voids in other peoples' lives and will come into the life of intelligent people like they came to fill the void.

They do this with love bombing and showering intelligent people with great attention. A vulnerable person will read no ulterior motive behind the attention they receive, particularly if the narcissist comes into their lives at the point where they are not feeling hopeful, maybe because of the loss of a dear one or some other kind of misfortune.

The problem with vulnerabilities is that even intelligent people might have a feeling of being manipulated, but these rational feelings are ignored because the narcissist is filling a particular need or longing.

Through degrading cycles of abuse, intelligent people may not realize that they are being tricked because their vulnerabilities may outweigh their intelligence.

5. Gaslighting narcissists have a lifetime's worth of training

Indeed, even the most intelligent of people can fall victim when they meet a narcissist. Narcissists are in general enchanting individuals who can trick even judges, law enforcement authorities and specialists.

Narcissists have always been the manipulators they are since childhood, and over time, they might have come to refine their manipulative tactics, so when they encounter intelligent people, they find it easy to capture them.

It is crucial to note that nobody is genuinely, ever totally invulnerable to being an object of abuse for a narcissist. The narcissist will get their way with intelligent people with:

1. *Twisted Truths.*

This is one of the most common ways that narcissists manipulate smart people. They either gloss over the truth, or they blatantly deny the truth. In a bid to get their needs met, it is shocking that they will go to any extent.

A narcissist will make a statement or a promise and deny it even in the same breath. They can pretend that the truth isn't what it is and conveniently put it on the smart people that it was an overreaction on their part, or a bad memory or a need for unnecessary drama.

2. Guilt-tripping.

Another thing narcissists love to do when they are gaslighting and manipulating intelligent people is to lay guilt on them. Guilt is a go-to tactic many narcissists uses without anyone realizing it. Guilt is very subtle, and a lot of times, even people outside the gaslighting situation won't see it.

The narcissist might perform a subtle action or say a phrase or hold their body in a certain way to keep the victim in check-in social situations. This keeps the victim in a constant state of anxiety and fear. The narcissist will deny if anything concerning the awkward behavior comes up in later conversation.

Narcissists are really good at making their victims believe they didn't experience what they did, or they made up something in their heads.

3. Kill the Messenger

Here is another thing narcissists do to gaslight and manipulate intelligent people: they ask smart people to "kill the messenger".

What does the phrase mean?

Narcissists, as controlling individuals, have a tendency to use other people as messengers or the mediators for some of the aspects of the victim's life.

Without concern for anyone involved, these abusive set of humans will use various people to send victims hurtful messages or to blame victims for their issues.

Many times, people will walk up to the victims and state that they are concerned about the victim's problems and will express themselves in a way everyone passing by will hear them. Most times, this leads to people coming around the victim and trying to offer support in genuine ways.

Unknown to the intelligent victim, these concerned individuals are just playing their parts in a script written by the narcissist.

So, what the narcissist is doing mostly is to employ "messenger" people who mean well and have no negative intention for the victim and tell them a lie that the victim is having a big problem. Of course, they are doing such things to deflect responsibility and further isolate and control their victims.

4. *Passive aggressiveness*

Narcissists are infamous for loving the passive-aggressive manipulation tactic. They have a knack for hitting victims where it hurts, and they will find and exploit the weak spots of intelligent people, so it's easier to make them feel guilty. This, of course, is where the narcissistic injury part comes in: the narcissist will then pretend to be the victim.

At the point of playing the victim, intelligent people feel sorry for them, and even if they don't feel sorry and go with the narcissist's charade, the narcissist will cry and whine and moan and act pathetic just to get what they want.

They will even go so far as to accuse intelligent people of being abusers, insensitive, mean and hateful. They project themselves onto the victim.

People are just extensions and objects to narcissists, even the people who are the closest to them. They literally do not care. They're users who don't mind using their friends and other family members to get what they want and to hurt others.

5. Fear and intimidation

The other tactic narcissists use on intelligent people is fear and intimidation. They might just resort to anger and threats in their words in order to manipulate and intimidate the victim. It is a well-known fact that narcissists are good at using anger and fear to coerce the people in their lives. They use threats and angry outbursts to make victims feel uncomfortable and upset

6. Head stepping

Another behavior a narcissist will use to manipulate you is what is called head stepping. A narcissist is very likely to belittle victims to try to bring them down to their own level. They are insecure people who feel threatened by intelligence and will use head stepping to make their victim bad in other people's eyes. The main goal of head stepping is to make the victim feel inferior and easier to control. They criticize you and tear down victims to make them feel inferior because by doing that it makes them feel superior.

Conclusion

Thank you for coming this far.

I want you to know that you (or someone you know) can make it to the other side to independence and freedom.

Gaslighting is the favorite tool of a narcissist, and a narcissist will seek to keep you under control by gradually eroding every bit of your sanity. Doubting your own senses is in no way healthy for you, and you have to be aware of how narcissists operate to avoid the mess of dealing with them in your future relationships.

Many people have fallen victims to narcissistic abuse in general and gaslighting to be more specific and have made it to the other side.

I wrote this book to help you find your own real voice against this special form of abuse (gaslighting), and I am cheering you on because I know what you have been through and what you are going through.

In this book, essential issues like identifying gaslighting behaviors and learning how to deal with the narcissist who seeks control were discussed in full detail. Cognitive dissonance and other effects of gaslighting acts were also discussed with concrete examples.

The effects of gaslighting might linger for a very long time in the psyche of victims, and as the saying goes, "prevention is better than cure". I have written this book so that you are fully aware of gaslighting as a manipulative tool and I hope you don't fall victim to this manipulative behavior.

Do not read this book alone and put it aside. Touch the lives of others with what you have learned, get copies for people you know are going through the ordeal and don't forget to provide all the support you can when you can.

In the event that you have been a victim at one time or you are just recovering from abuse, or you have just gained awareness that you are being manipulated with gaslighting in one of your relationships, I have discussed various ways of handling the situation in the book and I hope you learn a thing or two.

We live in the 21st century, a century which is famed for the advancements technology has brought, and we have seen how narcissists use smart devices in gaslighting and how they are increasingly picking up new tools to cause harm to people.

No one is immune to the tricks of narcissists, and even intelligent people can fall prey to gaslighting.

Also, we were able to take a journey away from the home and personal relationships to work and the community at large, as narcissists are a part of society and knowing how to deal with them wherever you encounter them is a skill you should seek to cultivate.

Earlier on in the introduction, I promised you an informative and enlightening book about gaslighting. I hope that the chapters of this book addressed every issue of concern of yours about gaslighting.

Millions and millions of people around the world are finding their real voice against gaslighting and are now enlightening more people about the damaging effects of gaslighting. It is no understatement when I repeat that countless people have fallen victim to this form of abuse at one point or the other in their lives.

The good news is there are countless survivors who have fought their way through depression and other devastating effects of gaslighting and are now living healthy lives. I believe that with the proper management techniques, any victim can get over the emotional abuse and mental manipulation to go on and lead a productive and fulfilling life.

My thoughts are with you, and you can find strength in the

fact that you can make it through the trying times. Use that strength to carry yourself through until you find your true self again.

You will make it eventually, I promise you. Know that you are not alone in dealing with gaslighting and emotional abuse.

The next step is to get all the help you can, find a support group, and start making plans for your own self.

So please, remember that Inner Strength + Emotional Support + Plan = Independence and Freedom.

You can do this.

I wish you the best of luck as you move forward to a happy chapter of your life.

Finally, if you have enjoyed this book, then I'd like to ask you for one little favor, would you be kind enough to leave a review for this book on Amazon?

Thank you, and good luck!

Made in the USA
Coppell, TX
21 January 2021

48579010R00079